Galatians

Galatians

Freedom through God's Grace

PHILLIP J. LONG

WIPF & STOCK · Eugene, Oregon

GALATIANS
Freedom through God's Grace

Copyright © 2019 Phillip J. Long. All rights reserved. Except for brief quotations in critical publications or reviews, no part of this book may be reproduced in any manner without prior written permission from the publisher. Write: Permissions, Wipf and Stock Publishers, 199 W. 8th Ave., Suite 3, Eugene, OR 97401.

Wipf & Stock
An Imprint of Wipf and Stock Publishers
199 W. 8th Ave., Suite 3
Eugene, OR 97401

www.wipfandstock.com

PAPERBACK ISBN: 978-1-5326-7120-3
HARDCOVER ISBN: 978-1-5326-7121-0
EBOOK ISBN: 978-1-5326-7122-7

Manufactured in the U.S.A.　　　　　　　　　　MAY 24, 2019

For Timothy F. Conklin, mentor and friend

Psalm 145:4

Contents

Preface | ix
Acknowledgements | xiii

1. Introducing Galatians | 1
2. One Gospel | 9
3. Paul and Judaism | 17
4. Paul and the Apostles | 27
5. The Antioch Incident | 37
6. Crucified with Christ | 48
7. Law and Faith | 60
8. Law and Promise | 72
9. Being Children of God | 84
10. Stop Acting Like a Slave | 91
11. Sarah and Hagar | 101
12. Freedom in Christ | 110
13. Life in the Spirit | 119
14. Doing Good to All | 135
15. Bearing the Marks of Jesus | 145

Bibliography | 155

Preface

WHAT KIND OF COMMENTARY IS THIS?

THIS BOOK IS A basic introduction to Paul's letter to the Galatians. There are hundreds of books available on Galatians already so it is important to explain my goals in this particular book in contrast to other styles of available commentary.

This is not an exegetical commentary. I do not comment on the Greek text nor do I try to solve every difficulty in the textual difficulty. Perhaps I will return to the text of Galatians and produce a more formal and scholarly commentary in the future, but the goals of this book preclude some of the more technical aspects of the letter. I rarely comment on Greek grammar except where it is critical to the meaning of a verse. While I do include some cultural and historical background in order to illuminate the text, I do not claim to be comprehensive in this area. There is far more to say about the background to Galatians than I cover in this book. There are several places in the book where I reflect some of the insights of the so-called "new perspective on Paul," but this book is neither a critique nor defense of this view of Paul's letters.

I do not intend for this book to be an expositional commentary, although that is the closest model. Expositional commentaries focus on an English translation and attempt to explain the details of the text. My goal is not necessarily the details but the overall point Paul makes in the letter. I will therefore move through Galatians in sections and comment on the most important aspects of each section in an attempt to understand what Paul is trying to say

Preface

both to the original readers and to Christians living in similar situations in the twenty-first century. I have made an effort to ground this contemporary application in the text of the Bible.

I intend this book for laymen, Bible teachers, and busy pastors who need an overview of the main issues in the book of Galatians. I envision this book being used in a small group Bible study or Sunday school class as a supplement to reading the letter to the Galatians. No book should ever be used to replace reading Scripture, but perhaps this book will help readers to better understand some of the nuances of Paul's thought in his letter to the Galatians.

STANDING ON SHOULDERS OF GIANTS

For the sake of the non-technical reader, I do not include many footnotes unless I directly refer to a source. This does not mean I did not read other commentaries and benefit from their insights. I list many of these in the bibliography.

These are the commentaries I found to be the most helpful as I worked through Galatians. Pride of place goes to F. F. Bruce's 1982 commentary in the NIGTC series. This is one of the best commentaries in terms of both exegetical insight and clarity. Bruce's student Ronald Y. K. Fung contributed a similar commentary to the NICNT series (Eerdmans, 1988). David A. deSilva's new volume in the NICNT series was published in late 2018, too late for me to read for this book. James Dunn's small commentary on Galatians (BNTC, 1993) is very readable and offers a view of Galatians from the "new perspective on Paul." I used *Grace in Galatia* by Ben Witherington III (Eerdmans, 1993) extensively when I first prepared notes on the letter for my Sunday evening series at Rush Creek Bible Church. Witherington's book has a wealth of background material drawn from the Greco-Roman world and I gleaned much from his commentary on Acts as well. Todd Wilson's *Gospel-Rooted Living* (Crossway, 2013) and Doug Moo's 2014 commentary in the Baker Exegetical Commentary on the New Testament were very helpful. Finally, Grant Osborne published his "verse-by-verse" commentary on Galatians in 2017, which has some of the same goals as this one. His commentary is a model of simplicity and a joy to read.

Occasionally I refer to historical texts in order to illustrate some aspect of first-century culture as it relates to Galatians. In the late first century Josephus retold the history of the Jews from the Old Testament through the Jewish rebellion against Rome in his *Antiquities of the Jews* (*Antiq.*). In addition, he wrote a more specific history of the Jewish rebellion against Rome, *The Jewish War* (*J.W.*). These two books are generally reliable works of history although Josephus had his own pro-Jewish agenda. This is also true for 1 Maccabees, a history of the Maccabean Revolt written in the mid-second century B.C. I cite apocryphal books like this in order to show what some Jews thought about their own traditions.

Acknowledgements

I NEED TO THANK Rush Creek Bible Church (Byron Center, Michigan), where I have taught through Galatians in both Sunday evening services and Sunday school classes. Both the board and staff of the church have been supportive of my teaching ministry since 2005 and RCBC is an excellent example of a church where the Bible is taught regularly. I have enjoyed many hours of discussions with people in our church on how to read and apply the Bible in general and the book of Galatians in particular. I owe a debt of gratitude to Timothy Conklin, who read the book and made many helpful suggestions. Jim Stringham also read through an early manuscript and suggested many improvements, as did my teaching assistants, Kyle Vegh, Kevin McKissick, and Zach Niles. I am thankful for their support and advice from all of these friends. I am responsible for any deficiencies in the final version of the book. Jerry Sterchi has been a conversation partner for many years and has helped me develop my thinking about Paul's letters. Finally, I must thank my students at Grace Christian University, who have endured many long lectures on these topics in my Pauline literature course and helped shaped the presentation of the book.

I

Introducing Galatians

WHY STUDY GALATIANS?

GALATIANS IS AN IMPORTANT book for Christians to study for several reasons. First, Galatians is one of the earliest of the Pauline letters and is therefore among the first documents written by Christians in the first century. Since I date the book before Acts 15, a study of Galatians helps illuminate the controversy in Acts 15 and allows us to see "behind the scenes" and hear firsthand how serious the problem was when discussed during that important conference in Jerusalem.

Second, Galatians deals with the first real controversy in the early church. In short, the book deals with the status of Jews and Gentiles in this present age and the application of the law of Moses to Gentiles. Paul argues quite passionately Gentiles are not "converting" to Judaism and therefore should not be expected to keep the law. Gentiles who accept Jesus as Savior are "free in Christ," not under the bondage of the Mosaic law.

Third, the book of Galatians deals with an important ramification of Paul's view of freedom in Christ. If Gentiles are not "under the law," are they free to behave any way they like? Does Paul's gospel mean Gentiles can continue to live like pagans and still be "right with God"? Obviously Paul does not promote a sinful lifestyle, so why should a Gentile convert live a righteous lifestyle? The answer is based on the believer's status as an adopted child of God who is free to serve God without compulsion.

Even though Galatians deals with a particular problem in the first century, the book is applicable to the present church. While Christian churches rarely demand obedience to the law of Moses, the idea of an unwritten law which defines a real "Christian" persists. Many churches exchange the idea of "freedom in Christ" with a series of beliefs and behaviors which (re)define what a Christian is. There is a growing trend in American evangelical churches to try and keep some of the law, especially Sabbath worship and the food laws. Galatians has a great deal to say to this developing movement.

GALATIANS AND THE BOOK OF ACTS

Of all the letters written by Paul, Galatians has generated the most discussion with respect to the recipients of the letter. There are several reasons for this. First, the letter is addressed to several churches in a region rather to a single church. For example, when Paul writes to Corinth, there is little doubt which city he had in mind or where to fit the book into the overall history found in the book of Acts. It is less clear where Galatians fits into Paul's ministry in Acts. Second, the geographical region "Galatia" shifted several times in the ancient world from an ethnic group to a Roman province. If the letter was addressed to ethnic Galatians, then the churches must be in the northern part of the region, near the Black Sea. But if the recipients were living in the Roman province of Galatia in the mid-first century, then the churches addressed were in what is now southern Turkey. Some of the earliest commentators on Galatians lived at a time when Galatia was referred to as a northern region.

This is not simply an academic question since it makes a difference in how we interpret the letter. Paul visited the southern area on his first missionary journey and established several churches there (Acts 13). He revisited each of these churches before returning to Antioch in order to report his success among the Gentiles (Acts 14:26–28). He may have passed through the northern region on his second journey but Acts does not state he ministered in the region or planted any churches. During his third missionary journey Paul visited part of the region, but again there is no record of planting churches. In Acts, Luke is rather general about what Paul did during this part of his ministry, so he may have planted churches even if Luke does not inform us. However, if the letter is written to the southern region, then this is the earliest of Paul's letters and reflects the first major conflict in the church: the status of Gentiles and the application of the law for believers in this age.

A PAULINE CHRONOLOGY

My suggested reconstruction of the circumstances of the letter looks like this. Paul encountered the risen Jesus on a mission to Damascus to arrest people who claim Jesus was the resurrected Messiah (A.D. 33–34; Acts 9). He immediately began to argue in the synagogues in Damascus that Jesus is the Messiah. There he faced both skepticism from the Jewish Christians, who were previously targets of his persecution, and also violent anger from those who saw Paul as a traitor.

Paul spent a period of time "in Arabia," likely in Damascus and the Nabatean Kingdom (now modern Saudi Arabia), most likely doing ministry among Gentiles and working out the implications of Jesus as a resurrected Messiah. I believe during these three years the Lord guided his reading and meditation on the Hebrew Bible to develop a rhetorical strategy for reaching Jews as well as Gentiles with the message of Jesus as Messiah. After these three years, Paul was forced to flee the region because king Aretas IV wanted to arrest him (2 Cor 11:32). Tensions between the Nabateans and Judea were high during this time and it is likely Paul was unable to continue living safely in the region, let alone preach a Jewish Messiah.

Paul then visited Jerusalem briefly to become acquainted with Jesus' disciples (Gal 1:18–22). This is his first time he met the apostles, but he only encounters Peter and James, the Lord's brother, who was not one of the original Twelve. After this meeting he returned to Syria and Cilicia, likely to his hometown of Tarsus. It is almost certain that he continued his ministry to Gentiles during this period.

The church at Antioch (in Syria) grew significantly, drawing both Jews and God-fearing Gentiles from the synagogues. Barnabas is sent from the Jerusalem church to ensure the church is developing correctly. Barnabas recognizes this as an opportunity for Paul, so he invites Paul to minister in Antioch. After some time in Antioch, the Holy Spirit sets Paul and Barnabas apart for a missionary trip to Cyprus and Asia Minor (Acts 13:1–3). During this "first missionary journey" Paul and Barnabas establish several churches in larger cities, mostly Roman colonies along Roman roads. These cities had significant Jewish populations and Paul was successful among the Jews, God-fearing Gentiles, and pagans.

After Paul's return trip to Antioch, teachers from Jerusalem visit Paul's churches founded on his first missionary journey and try to convince the Gentile converts to become Jews in order to be right with God. These Jewish teachers argue Gentiles must keep the whole law, beginning with circumcision. Paul argues with these opponent in Antioch (Acts 15:1) and then travels to Jerusalem to discuss the question with the apostles and elders (Acts 15:2–4). Paul likely wrote Galatians just prior to his visit to Jerusalem, although it is possible he wrote it just after the events of Acts 15. I will return to these details when I comment on Galatians 2.

It is important to understand the letter of Galatians was not Paul's first attempt to understand how the Mosaic law relates to Gentiles. Nor is Paul's mission to Galatia his first attempt to reach Gentiles with the gospel. By the time he writes the letter Paul has been targeting Gentiles in Arabia, Cilicia, and Antioch for more than twelve years. Galatians is therefore the fruit of many years of work and theological reflection on how Gentiles relate to grace of God demonstrated in Jesus Christ.

Introducing Galatians

MAIN THEMES OF GALATIANS

The main problem Paul addresses in the book of Galatians is the status of Gentiles in the church. Are Gentiles converting to Judaism? The immediate occasion for the letter appears to be that some teachers have arrived from Jerusalem claiming to have authority from James to require Gentiles to keep the law, beginning with circumcision. This Jewish party accepted Christ as Savior, but they continued to keep the law in addition to faith in Jesus. Paul calls this a "new gospel," although for Paul it is not really a gospel at all. It is possible these Jewish teachers were not even believers (Gal 1:6–7).

Another issue is Paul's authority to declare Gentiles free from the law. The Judaizers are likely questioning Paul's right to teach Gentile converts to not keep the Jewish law. They are asking, "Who is Paul? Where did he get his authority?" The first two chapters address this issue. This is a theme found from the very first lines of the letter, where Paul asserts he is an apostle by the authority of Jesus Christ and the Father himself (Gal 1:1–5).

In Galatians 2, Paul describes a conflict with Peter and admits "even Barnabas" has been led astray by the Judaizers. This is significant for Paul because he wants to establish his independence from Jerusalem, but also needs to maintain his authority as a full apostle commissioned by God. Paul must agree with his opponents that his authority does not derive from the apostles in Jerusalem or from James, the leader of the Jerusalem community. Paul agrees with them: he did not get his gospel of Gentile freedom from the apostles. But his admission does not imply he is inferior to the Jerusalem church in any way. His commission to be the apostle to the Gentiles comes directly from the resurrected and ascended Jesus.

A third issue in Galatians concerns the status of the law in the new age. If Paul has authority as the "apostle to the Gentiles," and if the Gentiles are really set free from the restrictions of the law, what was the point of the law in the first place? The purpose of the law is the concern of Galatians 3–4. It is likely a major part of the opponent's message concerning God's promise to Abraham (Gen 12:1–3). If someone wants to follow the God of Abraham and participate in the blessings of Abraham, Paul's opponents might argue, then like Abraham they must accept the sign of the covenant, which is circumcision.

In this section Paul reads the same texts his opponents might have used, Genesis 15:6 and 17:4–14. He develops the idea of the promise as foundation for the Mosaic law. To accept the sign of the covenant is to accept the whole covenant as fully realized in the law of Moses. Paul points out all who believe are sons of Abraham, but there were two sons of Abraham; one born to Sarah and one born to Hagar. His argument seems strange to modern readers since we are accustomed to seeing Isaac as the positive example and Ishmael as the negative. But in this case Paul argues the one born under the promise is obligated to the promise, the other son is not. Since Gentiles were not born under the promise nor were they part of the covenant people in the Old Testament, they are not now obligated to keep the law associated with the old covenant.

Finally, if Gentiles are free from the law, what is their motivation to behave in a moral and ethical way? When Paul taught Gentiles to not keep the law, did he also teach them they could live any way they chose? Not at all. Paul states very clearly that to "live by the Spirit" is not an opportunity for a libertine, sinful lifestyle. Paul addresses this problem in Galatians 5–6. His opponents may have thought by allowing Gentiles to be free from the law Paul was advocating freedom from all moral restraint. To a Jew, practices such as circumcision and food laws were foundational, but true ethical living was more important. The book of Proverbs, for example, teaches moral behavior without reference to the law. Was Paul claiming Gentiles who continued in a sinful lifestyle would be "saved" by believing in Jesus? Paul's opponents would consider this impossible.

Paul seeks to defuse this criticism of his Gentile mission by arguing Gentiles are free from the law of the old covenant, but now they live by a new law, the "law of Christ" (Gal 6:2). This new law is a law of love and is guided by the Holy Spirit. The "sin list" in

5:19–21 makes it clear Paul is not encouraging a kind of anarchist, libertine freedom. The life a Christ-follower lives in this present age is led by the Spirit of God as demonstrated by the "fruit of the Spirit" (5:22–23).

It is entirely possible Paul's congregations in Galatia struggled in two directions. Some seem to have developed a form of legalism which demanded keeping the law as a requirement for salvation. Others seem to have rejected any kind of moral restraint whatsoever and were behaving in ways inappropriate for members of the body of Christ. Paul's strongest condemnation (5:2–6:11) is reserved for those who were using their freedom to indulge in flagrant sinning.

CONCLUSION

Galatians is an intensely practical book. While it warns us against a legalistic religious experience, the letter does not embrace a sort of "anything goes" religion either. In fact, Paul is clear that believers in Christ are not converting to Judaism nor are they remaining pagans who accept some new philosophical idea. The Christ-follower has entered into a new life quite unlike either the old covenant or the pagan world.

QUESTIONS FOR FURTHER DISCUSSION

1. What are some examples of "Christian legalism" you have experienced?
2. How can religious legalism hinder spiritual growth?
3. Why would a Christian try to avoid moral responsibilities?

GALATIANS

ACTS AND GALATIANS: A PARALLEL CHRONOLOGY[1]

	Epistles	Acts
Paul as Persecutor	Gal 1:13–14	7:58; 8:1–3
Conversion	Gal 1:15–17	9:1–22 and parallels
In Arabia	Gal 1:17b	
Return to Damascus (after Three Years)	Gal 1:17c	
Flight from Damascus	2 Cor 11:32–33	9:23–25
First Visit to Jerusalem (Fifteen Days)	Gal 1:18–22	9:26–29
Ministry in Syria and Cilicia	Gal 1:21–22	9:30 (from Tarsus)
Possible Visionary Experience	2 Cor 12:1–10	
Ministry in Antioch (Possible Conflict with Peter)	Gal 2:11–14	11:25–26
Famine Visit to Jerusalem	Gal 2:1–10	11:29–30; 12:25
First Missionary Journey	Gal 4:13–15	13–14
Return to Antioch (Conflict with Peter)	Gal 2:11–14	14:26–28
Judaizers in Galatia	Gal 1:6–9; 3:1; 4:17—5:12; 6:12–13	Acts 15:1–2
Paul Writes Galatians from Antioch	Gal 6:11	
Paul and Barnabas Go to Jerusalem Council		15:2–29
Return to Antioch with Decree		15:30–35
Second Missionary Journey, Return to South Galatia		15:36—18:18

---

1. Chart based in part on Witherington, *Acts*, 445–59.

2

One Gospel

Galatians 1:1–10

INTRODUCTION

SOME FILMS ARE WELL-KNOWN for their iconic opening moments. The opening of *The Lion King* begins with a sunrise over an African plain with a Zulu chant in the background. The first few minutes of the movie provided important information the viewer needs in order to understand the film. Likewise, for people of a certain generation, the first few seconds of the first Star Wars film is still thrilling as the narrative background to the story crawls away from the viewer. In a similar way, the first few lines of Paul's letter to the Galatians are a foreshadowing of the most important themes of the letter. Paul begins by describing his own calling as apostle to the Gentiles before expressing his astonishment that his congregations in Galatia have turned away from the gospel he preached to them. The source of Paul's authority and the dangers of a false gospel form the main structure of Paul's letter.

GALATIANS

PAUL, AN APOSTLE (1:1–5)

Paul emphasizes his commission as an apostle from the very beginning of the letter. An "apostle" is someone who is sent as a representative of another, usually some kind of a group; an "ambassador, delegate, or messenger." Most scholars now associate the Greek word for *apostolos* with the Hebrew word *shaliach*. This word refers to a person who was sent as a representative or agent and acts with the same authority of the sending group. For example, the Jerusalem church sent Barnabas to Antioch in Acts 11:22 in response to the growth of the church there. Since he was sent as an official representative of the Jerusalem church, he could be called an "apostle." Barnabas could act as Jerusalem's representative in Antioch should questions arise. Verse 1 is therefore far more than Paul's signature on the letter: he is announcing a major theme of the book. Paul is not an apostle sent by the church of Antioch to the churches of Galatia, nor is he an agent sent out by the Jerusalem church. He is an apostle appointed by Jesus Christ and God the Father.

Living between the Ages

After greeting the church rather briefly, Paul expands on what he means by "Jesus Christ." Jesus is the one who "gave himself for our sins." This is perhaps an allusion to Mark 10:45: the Son of Man came to give his life as a ransom for many. In giving himself for our sins Jesus also set us free from this present evil age. The wording is reminiscent of Isaiah 53:5, 12 in the Greek Old Testament. It is possible Paul describes Jesus in this way because it was already familiar to his readers. Jesus has already provided salvation through his work on the cross and those who are in Christ are already saved out of the present evil age.

This "evil age" is a common way of describing the present time in Paul's letters as well as other Jewish first-century writings. In the Dead Sea Scrolls, for example, one important document calls the present age the "epoch of evil" (1QpHab 5:7) and the late-first-century Jewish apocalypse *4 Ezra* describes the present age as a time when Belial (Satan) is opposing God's will (7:12). Like these other Jewish writers, Paul is looking forward to a future kingdom. But he also thinks believers in Christ are already participating in the blessings of that future age. Paul contends we have already been rescued from this evil age.

For Paul, we live in a time "between the ages." Christ's death stands between the old covenant of the law and the future establishment of the kingdom of God. The book of Galatians is one of the earliest witnesses we have to what the first generation of Christians thought about the death of Jesus. It is clear from Acts the earliest followers of Jesus expected his return very soon (Acts 3:19–20). Paul believed some who are now alive may live until the return of the Lord (1 Thess 4:17). This "between the ages" perspective will be important later in the letter when Paul deals with observing the law in the present age.

Where's Barnabas?

Something is missing from the introduction of this letter. Paul normally includes others in the address of a letter (as in 1 Thess 1:1; 1 Cor 1:1). In this case he only includes his own name. Barnabas, the logical person to include, is missing. Where is Barnabas? Richard Bauckham suggested Paul did not include Barnabas because at the time of the writing of the letter he was still estranged from Paul.[1] When Paul and Barnabas returned to Antioch after planting several churches in Galatia, two things happened. First, men from James came to Antioch and objected to Peter sharing table fellowship with Gentiles. As a result, Peter and Barnabas withdrew from fellowship with Gentile believers, resulting in a stern condemnation from Paul (Gal 2:11–14). Second, Paul hears a report that Gentiles in his Galatia churches are also being pressured to keep the law, including circumcision. Barnabas accompanies Paul to Jerusalem to discuss the status of Gentles, and from the perspective

---

1. Bauckham, "Barnabas in Galatians."

of Acts 15 they seem to have reconciled. But it may be the rift goes deeper than either Galatians or Acts says. By the end of Acts 15 Barnabas and Paul part company. The issue there is the restoration of John Mark in a renewed mission to Gentiles.

While Bauckham does not say this, I think the presence of John Mark indicates Barnabas is unwilling to do Gentile ministry in the same way Paul does. The incident at Cyprus (Acts 13:4–12) is the key. John Mark leaves after Paul's dramatic condemnation of unbelieving Jews. In my view, John Mark is reacting to Paul's ministry to Gentiles who are not God-fearing Gentiles within the context of a synagogue. In addition, he may have disagreed with Paul over a gospel which did not require Gentiles to at least become God-Fearers, let alone allow them to break food or Sabbath traditions.

In addition, it is likely Barnabas was the leader of the first mission trip to Cyprus. At Lystra, Barnabas was thought to be Zeus (Acts 14:12), implying he was older and "in charge." Paul's actions on Cyprus and his sermon in Acts 13 make it clear his theology was going beyond reaching Gentiles who were already in the synagogue. By taking John Mark back as a travel companion (Acts 15:36–41), Barnabas may be signaling his unwillingness to minister outside of the synagogue in the way Paul does on his second missionary journey (Acts 16–17). Paul balances ministry in the synagogue with marketplace ministry, where he engages directly with Gentile philosophers (Acts 17).

Admittedly this is speculative, but Bauckham's reconstruction (and my slight extension of it) seems to explain the absence of Barnabas from the introduction of the letter. If Paul could say "even Barnabas agrees with me," he would likely have done so since this would have silenced his opponents. However, it appears he cannot claim the support of Barnabas at the time Galatians was written.

One Gospel

PAUL'S ASTONISHMENT (1:6–10)

Paul usually follows the address of a letter with a prayer of thanksgiving for the church. This is missing in Galatians. Paul's thanksgiving sections normally make some mention of the gospel and the joyful reception Paul received when he preached in the congregation. 1 Thessalonians, for example, has a ten-verse prayer; even in 1 Corinthians Paul recalls the church fondly in his opening prayer (1 Cor 1:4–9).

Instead of a prayer for the church, we have an extremely passionate condemnation of the church for so quickly abandoning the gospel they had received from Paul. It is astonishing to Paul that the church could so quickly be swayed by "another gospel." Since Paul has only recently evangelized the Galatian churches, the Judaizers must have followed behind Paul soon after his second pass through the region (Acts 14:24–28).

A False Gospel

The so-called gospel the Galatian believers are hearing is no real gospel at all. Paul calls those who are preaching this gospel "disturbers" or "agitators." The verb Paul uses refers to someone who changes allegiance from one political party to another. It appears in secular Greek to describe "Dionysius the Turncoat, who left the Stoics and adopted Epicureanism."[2] While this text is from the third century A.D., it illustrates how the word can be used for a defection away from one viewpoint to another. The modern parallel to the classic debates between "Calvinists vs. Arminians" is not a good analogy, since both sides in that debate are Christians using the Bible as a foundational text. In Galatians these are not Christian friends with a slightly different opinion on some minor theological point. The agitators are outside the umbrella of what it means to be Christian and the gospel they preach is not Paul's gospel at all. They are troublemakers who pervert the gospel so it is no longer the gospel Paul first delivered to Galatia. But the Galatians

2. Bauer et al., *Greek-English Lexicon*.

are not changing from one theological group to another; they are defecting from the one who called them. To follow the teaching of the Judaizers is to abandon God himself!

Paul states very clearly there is only one gospel and this gospel is the one he has already preached to the churches in Galatia. Paul is saying he has authority to say what the gospel is, or is not. The gospel he preached is *the* gospel and what the opponents are preaching is "*not* a gospel." They do not preach a legitimate variation on Paul's preaching nor are the agitators simply using a different method. Paul says they simply have understood the gospel wrong!

Let Him Be Accursed!

Paul is so committed to his gospel he pronounces a curse upon anyone who preaches a different gospel, including Paul himself! He makes a sweeping statement in verse 8: "Even if an angel preaches another gospel, do not believe it!" It is not the messenger that matters, but the content of the gospel they are preaching. If Paul himself were to return to Galatia and declare the Gentiles needed to keep the law, the churches should not listen to him.

That Paul should mention "an angel of the Lord" is important. Later in the letter Paul alludes to a Jewish tradition concerning the law given to Moses through the mediation of angels (Gal 3:19). If this tradition is in Paul's mind here, he claims that even if a new revelation were to be given in the same way Moses received the law but it contradicts his gospel, it must be rejected.

There is another hint about Barnabas being missing from the introduction. Paul says it does not matter who preaches the gospel. If anyone does not agree with the gospel Paul preached, they ought to be rejected, even if that person is someone as significant as Barnabas! It is possible Paul's opponents made something out of the fact Barnabas separated from table fellowship, perhaps claiming Barnabas was siding with them. But for Paul it does not matter who sides with him (or against him); his authority comes from directly from Jesus Christ.

One Gospel

To pronounce a curse is to say "let God's curse rest upon them." The idea of a "curse" in the Hebrew Bible is to place someone under "the ban." For example, in Joshua 6:17–18 the city of Jericho is under the ban, meaning the city was set aside for destruction. Paul is not cursing his opponents; he is asking God to deal with them severely. This curse is not a generic censure or a request for the opponents to leave the church. Paul is asking for God to judge them severely for preaching another gospel.

Paul's Harshness

Why is he so harsh on people teaching Gentiles to keep the law? F. F. Bruce suggests Paul knows law-keeping for salvation is a "snare and a delusion" from his own personal experience.[3] Paul had kept the law as perfectly as anyone, yet he knew he had not been completely faithful to God. In addition to the self-deception of law-keeping legalism, Paul knows there are dangerous implications for those Gentiles who try to keep the law. They risk placing their faith in something other than Jesus and the cross and therefore risk not really being saved.

This is possible, but it does not really take into account recent studies on Paul and Judaism. For example, the Pharisees did not really think keeping the law made one right with God. The Jew is "right with God" by election (God chose Israel), and the Jew stays right with God by keeping the law as best as he can. Not all Jews had to be Pharisees, but all Jews were expected to keep the key works of the law. Keeping the Sabbath, food laws, and circumcision were the principle boundary markers which defined a Jew. Paul's point is if the Gentiles try to keep these boundary markers, they will be no different than Gentile God-Fearers like Cornelius (Acts 10). A God-fearing Gentile worshiped in the synagogue and tried to keep the law without fully converting to Judaism. But for Paul, to acknowledge Jesus is to acknowledge that the law has been

---

3. Bruce, *Galatians*, 83

fulfilled in him as the Messiah and the believer in Christ is under no obligation to keep the law.

The gospel Paul preached unequivocally states God sent Jesus into the world to rescue those who stood condemned in this evil age. God did not send Jesus into the world to convert Gentiles to Judaism. Paul's gospel to the Gentiles is based on Jesus' sacrifice, but also means Gentiles are saved apart from the law. If they are converting to Judaism, then they are not really saved since the Jew also needs to accept the gospel of Jesus Christ.

CONCLUSION

The extreme harshness we detect is perhaps a product of our modern, Western multiculturalism. Nevertheless, Paul declares boldly there is only one gospel: his gospel. The other gospels are wrong (since they are not really the gospel). More importantly, by believing another gospel one may be prevented from being saved. This is therefore not a minor difference or a small theological distinction.

QUESTIONS FOR FURTHER DISCUSSION

1. Based on reading Galatians, describe the legalistic mindset of Paul's opponents.
2. What would motivate a Gentile Christian to want to keep the law?
3. How can legalism prevent a person from hearing the gospel of Jesus Christ clearly? Have you experienced this among Christians today?
4. What is a present-day example of a "false gospel" which may prevent someone from hearing the true gospel?

3

Paul and Judaism
Galatians 1:11–24

INTRODUCTION

AT THE BEGINNING OF the letter to the Galatians, Paul must clarify his relationship with the Jerusalem church. If Paul is under the authority of Jerusalem, then it is at least possible the "men from James" could claim Paul has not been authorized to preach a gospel to the Gentiles which sets them free from the Jewish law.

At issue here is not the core of the gospel message: "Christ died for our sins, was buried, and that he was raised on the third day, according to the Scriptures" (1 Cor 15:3–5). Paul clearly states this gospel was given to him as the primary core of the gospel. It is also clear the preaching of Christ crucified can be found in the apostolic preaching from the beginning of the book of Acts. Rather, Paul will argue in Galatians 1–2 is when the death and resurrection of Christ is applied to Gentiles they are not under the law. They are not converts to a form of Judaism. Rather, they are adopted children of God. Gentiles are not under the old covenant, Paul argues, so they are free from the law.

Paul's law-free gospel for the Gentiles focuses on the finished work of Christ on the cross. It is only the cross that can provide people with right standing before God. As Ben Witherington observes, "this distinctive gospel message about Christ Paul admits is not the sort of thing human beings could have come up with on their own. It had to be revealed by God for it to be known at all."[1] Paul's point is not that the law is bad or there is something wrong with the Judaism in which he was raised, but that he has received a revelation from Jesus Christ himself explaining what God is doing in the present age.

PAUL'S GOSPEL WAS REVEALED TO HIM BY JESUS CHRIST (1:11-12)

From the beginning of this letter Paul speaks in first-person pronouns. He is not writing on behalf of a ministry team as he did in 1 Thessalonians or 1 Corinthians. Paul is presenting his own testimony about how he encountered the grace of God. First, Paul claims he was not evangelized by other apostles. We know from Acts Paul was in fact a bitter opponent of the apostolic message. He first came into contact with the gospel in the Synagogue of the Freedmen, where Stephen was preaching (Acts 6:8–10), and he heard Stephen's sermon before the Sanhedrin (Acts 7:57–58). Second, Paul claims he did not learn his gospel from the other apostles. After his encounter with Jesus, Paul did not have a period of discipleship with a mentor in order to learn the basics of the gospel. In fact, he says he did not encounter the apostles until well after he was given a revelation from Jesus.

Paul may consider himself a paradigm of the grace of the gospel since he was absolutely opposed to the apostles until he encountered the risen Jesus on the road to Damascus. He considers himself "abnormally born" and the least of the apostles (1 Cor 15:8–9) and the "chief of sinners" (1 Tim 1:15). Until he encountered Jesus on the road to Damascus, Paul was completely opposed to the preaching of a crucified Messiah.

---

1. Witherington, *Grace in Galatia*, 92.

A Revelation from Jesus

The origin of Paul's gospel to the Gentiles is a revelation from Jesus (Gal 1:12). The word "revelation" appears in Paul's letters thirteen times, and, as might be expected, it has the connotation of God's decisive actions in history to bring salvation into the world. For example, the word is the title of the final book of the New Testament, the "Revelation of Jesus Christ." Paul does not say he developed his law-free gospel through careful reading of the Hebrew Bible nor does he claim to have discovered some new way of reading the Old Testament to prove Gentiles should not keep the law. Paul's audacious claim is Jesus revealed this teaching to him through some sort of apocalyptic vision.

This is not the only time Paul makes this claim. In Ephesians 3:1–6 Paul says he received this law-free gospel for the Gentiles as a "mystery kept hidden" until God revealed it to him. This "revelation of a mystery" stands in contrast to Paul receiving a tradition from the other apostles. In 1 Corinthians 15:3 Paul says he passed along to the Corinthians what he received from the apostles. In contrast to this passing along of tradition, Paul claims in Galatians 1:12 he was not informed by others of his "law-free gospel" for the Gentiles; God revealed it to him through Jesus.

Paul now begins to offer evidence for the claim his gospel does not come from anyone other than God. If it is true his commission and law-free gospel are from God, then the Galatian believers are in danger of missing the gospel if they choose to exchange it for the "gospel" taught by Paul's opponents.

PAUL'S REPUTATION IS EVIDENCE (1:13–17)

The churches of Galatia undoubtedly knew of Paul's reputation before they had heard him preach the gospel. Paul admits in 1:13 people had heard of his reputation (cf., Phil 3:6). However, while they might have known about his life as a persecutor of the church, the church would not have known much about the years after his conversion and before he evangelized their region.

Zealous for His Traditions

By Paul's own admission, he was zealous in the task of exterminating the new Christians. This violent past may have been a source of difficulty for Paul. If there were people in the Galatian churches who doubted Paul's authority to the point they would reject his gospel, they may have pointed to his persecution of the church as proof Paul was not to be trusted. Describing his persecution of the earliest believers, Paul says he was "zealous for his task" (1:13). Zeal can be good or bad, but in this case Paul's zeal was misguided. As N. T. Wright reminds us, zeal in the first century was something radical and rebellious, something "done with a knife."[2]

Several Jewish heroes of the faith were "zealous" for the law and used violence to deal with extreme breaches of law. Phinehas, for example, burned with zeal and killed an Israelite who was grossly violating the law by bringing a prostitute of Baal to the tabernacle (Num 25:6–13). Closer to the time of Paul, the priest Mattathias "burned with zeal" when he ignited the Maccabean revolt (1 Macc 2:19–27). As James Dunn observes, "such zeal was characteristically directed towards the preservation of Israel's purity and distinctiveness."[3]

Paul stood within this tradition of zealous defense of the traditions of the fathers (1:14). The traditions he has in mind are the way the Pharisees in particular understood the law. Jesus frequently came into conflict with the Pharisees over the "traditions of the elders." In Mark 7:5, for example, the Pharisees complain Jesus does not follow their traditions concerning ceremonial washing of hands before a meal.

This is an example of the kind of tradition Paul excelled in as a Pharisee, but it does not explain his violence toward the followers of Jesus. Paul's main concern was what the growing Jesus movement was saying about the Messiah. For a Pharisee, Jesus could not be the Messiah since he had been executed and "hung on a tree." The early Jewish followers of Jesus were not reaching out to

---

2. Wright, *What Saint Paul Really Said*, 27.
3. Dunn, *Galatians*, 61.

Gentiles yet, nor does it appear they were encouraging Jews to give up keeping the law. As far as Acts 1–8 is concerned, the apostles continued to be a movement within Judaism, even if they understood Jesus was the Messiah.

In addition to his zeal, Paul claims he had excelled at the practice of Judaism more than any others in his age group (1:14). The word for his development in religion is the same word applied to Christ in Luke 2:52; he "grew in wisdom and stature." Paul may be referring to his age contemporaries or his social equals (other Pharisees). Paul is boasting about how quickly he advanced through the religious ranks. Paul highlights two things in Galatians 1:14: he was born a Jew and he excelled in the practice of Judaism more than others. Paul says he was part of the old covenant by birth and he was doing everything required to stay a part of the covenant.

What Gets You In, What Keeps You In

As Ed Sanders has said, Second Temple–period Judaism was about election (what got you in) and practice (what kept you in).[4] For Paul, neither of these things matter anymore. Simply being born a Jew does not make one right with God (via God's gracious national election) nor do the distinctive practices of Judaism keep one right with God. Only the grace of God as revealed through the death and resurrection of Jesus can provide forgiveness of sin through justification by faith. Ethnic identity does not matter to Paul in the present age, whether Jew or Greek.

Paul is laying the foundation for a discontinuity between the people of God in the old covenant and the people of God in the new covenant. As we will see, some members of the Jerusalem church disagree with Paul and argue there is continuity between the people of God. The new covenant is for New Israel, they might have claimed, and if Gentiles come into the new covenant they must do so as New Israel.

4. For a brief overview of Sanders and the New Perspective on Paul, see Long, "Brief Introduction."

CHOSEN BEFORE BIRTH

Paul was chosen for his role as an apostle before he was born (1:16). If ever there was an individual who did not deserve the office of apostle, it would have been Paul! There is some subtle wordplay in this verse. Paul describes himself as "set apart," the root meaning of the word "Pharisee," a "separated person." Paul may be saying, "I was a separated person, but now God has made me truly separated." This language is similar to the call of the prophets Jeremiah and Isaiah (Jer 1:5; Isa 49:1–6). In fact, Jeremiah was also separated to be a prophet before birth. This is remarkably similar to Paul's claim here in Galatians.

Commissioned to Preach the Gospel to the Gentiles

God called and commissioned Paul to preach the gospel of God's grace among the Gentiles. Before Paul was called by God in Acts 9, the gospel of Christ crucified had only been preached to Jews. Even though the Jerusalem church had begun to move into Judea, they still focused their efforts on Jerusalem and on people who were Jewish. It is not until after Paul's calling that Peter grudgingly goes to Cornelius, a Gentile who already practiced Judaism, so that faithfully God sent Peter to him (Acts 10:1–6). There seems to be a change in God's program after Paul's calling to be the apostle to the Gentiles.

The reason for this change in God's program is to be traced to the beginning of Acts. When the gospel was first preached, it was preached to the Jews in Jerusalem who were going to worship in the temple. Peter explicitly states if the Jews listen and repent of the sin of rejecting the Christ, God will send the Messiah and the "times of refreshing" promised by the prophets will come (Acts 3:19–20). As the story unfolds in Acts, this offer was systematically rejected by the Jewish leadership by arresting Peter and John and ultimately killing Stephen (Acts 7). It is only after this rejection that Paul is appointed to be the light to the Gentiles (Acts 9). Even though Philip was sent to the Ethiopian (a convert to Judaism,

Acts 8) and Peter preaches to Cornelius (a God-fearing Gentile, Acts 10), the gospel was still only being preached to those who were converting in some way to Judaism.

Paul says he did not confer with the apostles in Jerusalem after his conversion (Gal 1:17). The word "confer" describes the process of coming to someone, presenting a problem, and getting advice or instructions based on that meeting. Paul did not go to anyone for instruction in the gospel; he did not take his revelation and share it with others and get their opinion before he preached. He began to preach the gospel right away in Damascus and presumably Arabia. In fact, Paul says he did not go to Jerusalem for three years and even when he did he met with only Peter and James (1:18–20). For Paul, his apostleship is based on the fact he has seen the risen Savior and has been given a direct commission from the Lord to preach to the Gentiles. The opinions concerning this from those who are already apostles do not matter to Paul at all.

In summary, what Paul is trying to communicate to his readers is that he did not receive his instruction from Jerusalem after his conversion nor did he receive any kind of commission or permission from them to do his ministry. He is a completely independent apostle appointed directly by God.

PAUL AND THE JERUSALEM CHURCH (1:18–24)

The word "next" in verse 18 indicates Paul is setting up a time frame for these events. He does not want anyone to accuse him of leaving out events. The visit Paul makes here is to Jerusalem for a short time only and is by no means a "formal" conference. This is likely the visit recorded in Acts 9:26–30.

Paul's First Meeting with Jerusalem

Paul says he met only with Peter and James, the brother of Jesus (1:18–19). When Paul comes to Jerusalem, Peter is still the primary leader of the Jerusalem church. But by Acts 15 James appears in charge of the meeting and it is James who sends a letter to the churches clarifying how Gentiles relate to the law. From the reference to James in Galatians it is unclear whether Paul considered him to be an apostle or not. Not everyone who saw Jesus resurrected was an apostle. But James may have been given a special commission by the resurrected Jesus. 1 Corinthians 15:7 says Jesus appeared to James. Since there are only three individuals named in 1 Corinthians 5:3–8 (Peter, James and Paul), it is possible each of the three were given a special commission for ministry from the resurrected Jesus.

What did Paul, Peter, and James do in this meeting? The Greek here is clear. Paul states he went to Jerusalem to "interview" Peter. In Hellenistic Greek this word refers to making someone's acquaintance. Paul wanted to meet Peter, perhaps to let him know how he too had seen the resurrected Jesus. By selecting this word to describe the meeting, Paul is saying he was not submitting to the apostles nor was he seeking approval for his mission to the Gentiles. Remember this meeting is three years after Paul's conversion on the road to Damascus and he had been obedient to his call from the very beginning. Perhaps this was an opportunity for Paul to learn something of Jesus' life and teaching as well as some of the traditions used among the earliest followers of Christ (1 Cor 15:3–5).

The reference to James may also indicate Paul was interested in meeting as many people who had known Jesus as possible. Certainly meeting Jesus' own brother would have been of interest to Paul. In addition, this may be a hint James was already influential over the more conservative Jewish Christians in the Jerusalem church. If this is true, by meeting both Peter and James Paul would be meeting with the leaders of two important groups in the Jewish church.

Paul says they only met for fifteen days, but this would have been plenty of time for Peter to tell Paul a great deal about Jesus and his earthly ministry. This firsthand interview allowed Paul to gather facts from eyewitnesses of Jesus' teaching. In another early letter, Paul alludes to Jesus' teaching on the Mount of Olives (1

Thess 5:1–3, cf. Matt 24:42–44). This first meeting may have been the source of Paul's knowledge of Jesus' teaching.

After the Meeting

It is clear from Galatians 1 Paul's first contact with Jerusalem was minimal. He only saw a few people who might be considered the leadership of the Jerusalem church. More important for the argument of the first two chapters of Galatians, the meeting was in no way a confirmation of his call or a time of instruction. He concludes by saying, "with God as my witness, I am not lying." This oath conforms to Roman tradition in swearing the truth. Paul considers himself in a courtroom, swearing a legally binding oath that he is indeed telling the truth.

After his brief visit with Peter, Paul sets out for the Roman province of Syria and Cilicia, likely to continue his ministry in his hometown of Tarsus. According to Acts, Paul boarded a ship for Tarsus (9:30) and later was invited to Antioch by Barnabas (11:25–26). This period is similar to his time in Nabatean Arabia, where he preached the gospel to Gentiles. Paul seems to have had more success since news of him reaches the believers in Judea. The "churches of Judea" contains those who were scattered from Jerusalem in Acts 8:1 as a result of Paul's persecution.

At the time of Paul's first visit to Jerusalem, the church at Jerusalem was very small and many of the original converts were scattered by Paul's persecution (Acts 8:1–3). These churches knew nothing about Paul other than that he was the one who had persecuted them and he was now preaching the gospel.

CONCLUSION

From the very beginning of the letter Paul wants to demonstrate he is the apostle called by the resurrected Jesus and commissioned by God directly to go to the Gentiles. His opponents in Galatia may have made a great deal out of his dark past as a persecutor of the church, but Paul is open and honest about his former zeal. Prior to his first missionary journey, he had very little contact with Jerusalem and he did not consider himself operating under their commission or their orders. If "men from James" are causing trouble in Galatia, they cannot claim to have more authority than Paul since Paul's commission is directly from the Lord.

QUESTIONS FOR FURTHER DISCUSSION

1. In what way is Paul's claim to have received a revelation from God similar to Old Testament prophets?
2. Paul claims to have been the "chief of sinners," yet God chose him to be his apostle to the Gentiles. How is Paul's salvation and ministry an example of God's grace?
3. Does Paul's independence as an apostle have any ramifications for reading other parts of the New Testament?

4

Paul and the Apostles
Galatians 2:1–10

INTRODUCTION

GALATIANS 2:1–10 DESCRIBES A meeting between Paul and the "pillars" of the Jerusalem church. Paul brought Titus to this meeting as an example of what God was doing through his ministry. Titus was a Gentile, a former pagan, who was accepted into the body of Christ by the grace of God through faith. He was not a God-fearing Gentile who accepted God's grace through faith but still kept some of the boundary markers of the law. Paul puts the question to the pillars of the Jerusalem church: "What are you going to say about Titus? Should he be circumcised or not?"

Paul must balance two things in his report of this meeting. On the one hand, he needs to show the Galatian churches he is not under the authority of the Jerusalem church. Paul's opponents in Galatia question Paul's authority to teach that Gentiles are free from the law. But he also must demonstrate that his preaching among the Gentiles is accepted also by Jerusalem. When Peter and James had an opportunity to correct him, they did not. In fact, the Jerusalem leaders agreed with Paul and did not compel the Gentile convert Titus to be circumcised.

Galatians

GALATIANS 2 AND ACTS

With respect to the book of Acts, when does this meeting take place? Paul says it was "after fourteen years" (2:1) but there are three possibilities for understanding this phrase. First, it may refer to the time since Paul's conversion. Galatians 2:1–10 would therefore refer to the brief "famine visit" (Acts 11:29–30). Luke tells us in that passage Barnabas and Paul delivered a gift from Antioch to help the poor believers in Jerusalem in response to a prophecy from Agabus. Paul says in Galatians he went to Jerusalem because of a revelation (2:1) and he was told to continue to remember the poor (2:10). "Remembering the poor" in Jerusalem is exactly what the famine relief visit intended to do. However, a serious problem for this position is that Acts 11:29–30 does not mention a meeting with any of the leaders in the Jerusalem church, whether public or private.

A second possibility is this event takes place "after fourteen years" from the last time referenced in Galatians, Paul's three years in Arabia. This would mean the visit took place seventeen years after his conversion. Galatians 2:1–10 would therefore be Paul's report of the meeting in Acts 15. This meeting, usually called the "Jerusalem conference," discussed the relationship of Gentiles and the law. There are several problems with this view. In Acts 15, Paul does not go to Jerusalem in response to a revelation. He is responding to some teachers in Antioch who are arguing Gentiles must submit to circumcision. Second, there is no reference to Titus in Acts 15, although Titus is not mentioned at all in Acts. Third, the meeting in Acts 15 seems public: "the apostles and elders gathered." In Galatians 2:2 Paul specifically states he met privately with those who were "influential." Fourth, while the issue in both Acts 15 and Galatians 2:1–10 is circumcision of Gentile believers, Paul does not refer in Galatians to the decision of the conference or the letter drafted by James. It is true James told Paul to continue to remember the poor, but he has already been doing so for some time before Acts 15.

A third possibility is Paul went to Jerusalem on another occasion and met with the leaders of the Jerusalem church. This would mean Galatians 2:1–10 does not refer to either Acts 11:29–30 or Acts 15. If that is the case, Paul does not mention the famine visit in the letter. It is possible he did not need to since he did not meet with any leaders at that time. This could potentially be a problem if his opponents pointed out Paul had more contact with Jerusalem than he admitted in his letter, but Paul is only interested in detailing visits with the church pillars, not all of his visits to the city of Jerusalem.

All things considered, I think the third option is best for understanding this meeting in Galatians 2:1–10. At some time prior to Acts 15, perhaps even before his first missionary journey, Paul met with Peter and James in order to establish a precedence for Gentiles who accept Jesus as Savior. Paul's success among the Gentiles created a class of believers who were neither ethnically Jewish nor converts to Judaism (or near-converts like Cornelius). At the time of this meeting, Peter and James agreed these Gentiles were not converting to a form of Judaism and were therefore not required to keep the old covenant.

PAUL MET PRIVATELY WITH THE LEADERS IN JERUSALEM (2:1–3)

Paul states he went up to Jerusalem in response to a "revelation." In Acts 11, Agabus, a prophet in Antioch, predicted that the famine would be severe. It is possible the Antioch church responded by saving supplies prior to the beginning of the famine and them shared then with Jerusalem. Paul therefore refers to the prophecy of Agabus as a revelation. But it is also possible this was a revelation given directly to Paul.[1] The earlier use of this word in Acts does in fact refer to a revelation given directly to Paul. A personal revelation also helps Paul's argument to say God directly commanded him to go to Jerusalem to deal with the problem of circumcision

---

1. Bruce, *Galatians*, 108.

of Gentile converts. In either case, Paul was not summoned to Jerusalem by the apostles to present his gospel for approval. He only went to the pillars after a revelation from God.

Setting His Gospel before the Apostles

For Paul, the point of this visit is to set before the apostles his gospel which he is already preaching among the Gentiles. To "set a matter before another" is to "lay out a case." The word appears in Acts 25:14 in the context of a legal matter and it is often used with the "connotation of request for a person's opinion."[2] The problem for Paul is that he was commissioned directly by Jesus to preach this gospel to the Gentiles and he believes he does not need to submit to the authority of the Jerusalem church. However, some believers in Jerusalem disagree with his gospel ("men from James," Gal 1:12). It is possible these opponents question Paul's commission from God to teach Gentiles they do not have to keep the law. While Paul does not need Jerusalem's approval, he does need their blessing in order to keep the more conservative side of this disagreement in check. This will be an increasingly difficult problem as Paul has more success among pagan Gentiles as opposed to God-fearing Gentiles.

Who Is Titus?

Paul brings Titus with him as a "test case" for the apostles. Should a Gentile convert named Titus be circumcised after he has accepted Jesus as Savior? Who is this Titus? In 2 Corinthians 8:23 Titus is identified as one of Paul's coworkers and the representative sent to the Corinthian church to deal with certain problems in Paul's absence (2 Cor 12:18). That Paul calls him a Greek indicates he is ethnically a Gentile as opposed to a Hellenistic Jew. Paul does not describe him as a God-fearing Gentile. It is likely Titus was a convert from paganism rather than a Gentile who was worshiping

---

2. Bauer et al., *Greek-English Lexicon*.

in the synagogue, like Cornelius. When Paul writes the letter of Galatians, Titus was already a coworker in his ministry and therefore is an excellent example to bring to Jerusalem. He is a Gentile who exhibits the presence of the Holy Spirit in his life and one who has committed his life to the ministry of preaching the gospel of Jesus Christ to the Gentiles.

By this point in the story of the early church, Paul had already reached significant numbers of pagan Gentiles with the gospel. The Galatian churches are the chief example of his success. While Peter visited Cornelius in response to a vision from God, the Jerusalem church may not have targeted God-fearing Gentiles. The Antioch church, on the other hand, did reach out to God-Fearers and may have begun to extend their preaching to other socially connected Gentiles. Once again, Paul is on the extreme edge of the developing church since he has been called to reach out to Gentiles, whether they were worshiping in the synagogue or not. A Gentile like Titus accepted Jesus Christ as Lord and Savior and would not have been living in accordance with Jewish practice and tradition.

According to Paul, James and Peter agreed that it was not necessary for Titus to be circumcised (2:3). He clearly accepted Jesus Christ as Savior by "grace through faith." Titus did not convert to Judaism, therefore he does not need to be circumcised or keep the law. Titus is consequently an example of a Gentile who is right with God yet also free from the law.

SOMEONE "SLIPPED IN" TO INVESTIGATE (2:4–5)

It appears there were some in the Jerusalem church who did not agree with this decision. Paul calls these people "false brothers" who have spied on the meeting with the intention of imposing law on the Gentiles. The language Paul uses is military and political. These false brothers are "undercover agents and conspirators."[3] It seems most likely the false brothers are similar to the "men from

---

3. Witherington, *Grace in Galatia*, 136

James" in Galatians 2:12 or the "priests and Pharisees" mentioned in Acts 15:1. Although they were committed to Jesus as the Messiah, they remained Jewish believers who believed the church was a reform movement within Judaism. They would have considered Paul's gospel dangerous because it allowed people to become a part of this Jesus movement who were not fully committed to preparing for the return of the Messiah.

Whoever these people were, they found a way to intrude on the meeting between Paul and the apostles with the intention of causing trouble for Paul. That they intend to "bring us into slavery" indicates they will insist Gentiles be circumcised and fully keep the law as a Jew if they are to be full members of the messianic community. The early Jewish Christian movement had extremely vibrant messianic hopes. Acts 2–3 indicates the community really expected Jesus to return as Messiah immediately. If this was the case, it is possible some within the Jerusalem community saw an uncircumcised Gentile as a threat to the purity of the messianic community.

Insisting on Circumcision

Who would have insisted Titus submit to circumcision? Apparently these false brothers believed Gentiles were actually converting to Judaism. If this is the case, then they ought to be circumcised and be obedient to the law. If they are accepting the gospel by faith just like Abraham, then they ought to be circumcised just like Abraham. In the first century there was a debate within Judaism concerning Gentile conversion and the need for circumcision. Josephus illustrates this debate with the story of Helena, queen of Adiabene, and her son Izates, who "changed their course of life, and embraced the Jewish customs" (Josephus, *Antiq.* 20.2.4). In this story, Izates feels he ought to be circumcised in order to be a "true convert." Two rabbis visit Izates in order to give him advice on this decision. One rabbi insists the man be circumcised in order to convert to Judaism, but the other argues there are some cases in which circumcision would not be required. In Galatians, the false brothers also insisted any convert to Judaism must accept the Abrahamic sign of the covenant.

Why Now?

It is odd this issue came up fourteen years after Paul's conversion. What changed to make the issue of Gentile circumcision so controversial? James Dunn suggests the first Gentile converts (like Cornelius) were God-fearers and therefore already more or less an "exception" in the synagogue.[4] Gentiles were already keeping most of the boundary markers and were likely as ritually pure as any of the Jewish members of the synagogue, with the exception of circumcision. As long as there were only a few exceptional Gentile converts, the issue of circumcision was unlikely a matter of concern. But as more Gentiles came to Jesus and were worshiping in churches alongside Jewish Christians, at least some Jews began to wonder about the status of a Gentile convert before God. Are they really part of the messianic community if they are not circumcised? At least the Pharisees mentioned in Acts 15:5 thought they were not.

Going beyond Dunn's suggestion, it is possible the story of Izates is a model for the debate within the emerging church in Galatians 2. Some, like Paul, insisted circumcision was not required for Gentiles, while others (the Pharisees in Acts 15:5) insisted it was. What set Paul apart from the other apostles was his commission to go directly to the Gentiles. This means he specifically targeted non-God-fearing Gentiles, like the Roman governor of Cypress, Sergius Paulus (Acts 13:4–12). Paul was going to "real pagans," so to speak. If Cornelius was not compelled to be circumcised because he was close enough to Judaism, what about someone like Titus? He was not keeping the Sabbath and food laws when he came to Christ. The Jerusalem leaders agreed with Paul: Titus did not need to be circumcised since circumcision would indicate he had converted to Judaism.

There likely was a confrontation between Paul and this third party who insisted on Gentiles converting to Judaism. Paul states

4. Dunn, *Beginning from Jerusalem*, 445–56.

he "did not yield to his opponents for a moment" (2:5). The language Paul chose to use here to describe his own actions is clear. He was attacked in some way and he did not compromise his position in the least. The third group put pressure on Paul to have Titus circumcised and therefore "convert" to Judaism. Paul strongly argued the gospel did not demand Gentiles keep the law. For Paul, there could be no compromise on this. Paul's motivation for this defense of the gospel is any modification of the gospel already preached to the Galatians is a false gospel. If anyone, including Paul himself, preaches a different gospel, then it is a false gospel (Gal 1:3–5).

THE APOSTLES ADD NOTHING TO PAUL'S GOSPEL (2:6–10)

Paul says the pillars "added nothing" to him (2:6). This can be taken in two different ways. First, the pillars did not add anything to Paul's gospel, meaning they "approved" of the gospel Paul was teaching and did not require him to include something more in his preaching to the Gentiles. Second, this may mean the approval of the apostles did nothing to enhance Paul's honor or prestige, since he was already commissioned by God to preach this gospel.[5] In the context, Paul's dismissal of the honor of the apostles indicates he did not require their approval and it did not matter if they agreed with him or not since he knew he was right. This might be something like a doctor who has an MD getting an approval to practice medicine from a local high school. The approval of Jerusalem does not matter to Paul since a higher authority has already given him all approval he needs.

The Right Hand of Fellowship

The pillars give Paul the "right hand of fellowship." Does this indicate some sort of formal agreement? The "giving of a hand" is found in the Hebrew Bible several times (2 Kgs 10:15 for example).

---

5. Witherington, *Grace in Galatia*, 140.

In general, this is an offer of friendship between equals, but occasionally it is a gesture from a superior person to a socially inferior person. Giving the "right hand" is ambiguous. It is possible Paul understood this gesture as friendship between equals, but perhaps the apostles understood it as friendship with an inferior, Paul. Whatever the case, Paul takes the presence of the opponents in the Galatia churches as a breach of this agreement.

Was the agreement a "division of labor"? Peter will go to the Jews while Paul goes to Gentiles? It may be the division was ethnic or geographical. According to 1 Peter, Peter ministers in northern Asia Minor. 1 Corinthians implies Peter had some influence in Corinth, but this may not imply he actually ministered in that city. It is likely Peter continued doing the sort of ministry Acts 10–12 describes. Like Jesus, Peter seems to have ministered primarily to the Jews, but especially to those on the fringe of Judaism. James seems to have remained in Jerusalem ministering to Jews who remained faithful to the law (Acts 21:20).

Paul, on the other hand, continued to go to synagogues as a part of his regular pattern of ministry (Philippi, Thessalonica, Berea, and Corinth), and in 2 Corinthians 11:24 Paul indicates he had been disciplined in the synagogue several times before A.D. 52. But Paul did avoid regions which were already evangelized by others; his intention was always to move west into regions which had not yet heard the gospel (Rom 15:23–24).

Remember the Poor

At the private meeting Paul was encouraged to "remember the poor." The "poor" in mind here are the members of the Jerusalem church, the very people the famine visit was intended to help. The Jerusalem church appears to be still living in a sort of shared community, supported by gifts. Ben Witherington suggests this famine was complicated by a Jubilee year.[6] If this was the case, the poor believers in Jerusalem were even more dependent on Antioch than

---

6. Witherington, *Acts*, 429.

ever. Witherington wonders if the handshake was an agreement to continue the financial relief arrangements between the Antioch church and the Jerusalem church.

CONCLUSION

The meeting Paul describes in Galatians 2:1–10 concerns the status of Gentiles: are they really converts to Judaism, and if so, should they submit to circumcision? Paul's point in telling his side of the story is to demonstrate that the Jerusalem church saw nothing wrong with his gospel and did not require Titus to be circumcised. The meeting was between the core leadership of the Jerusalem community: Peter, James, and John. But there was another party present, a third party who insisted the Gentiles were in fact converting to Judaism. It is this third party who are questioning Paul's law-free gospel. The issue in Galatians 2:1–10 is circumcision, but in 2:11–21 Paul must deal with another problem for Jews and Gentiles in churches: sharing food with Gentiles.

QUESTIONS FOR FURTHER DISCUSSION

1. Paul says in 1 Corinthians 9:20, "to the Jews I become as a Jew" in order to reach the Jews with the gospel. How do you think Paul did this? In what ways did he "become as a Jew" when presenting the gospel to the Jewish people in the synagogue?

2. In what ways can Paul's meeting with James, Peter, and John be used as a model for resolving conflict between Christian brothers and sisters?

5

The Antioch Incident
Galatians 2:11–14

INTRODUCTION

ALTHOUGH IT IS EMBARRASSING when someone is accused of hypocrisy, most people enjoy it when a famous person is found to not "practice what they preach." We seem to relish it when an actor speaks out against the oil industry and then is caught vacationing on the yacht of a Middle Eastern oil billionaire. The press loves the scandal of a family-values politician caught in an adulterous affair. Despite our human tendency to obsess on salacious details, it is always disheartening when a Christian is caught acting like a hypocrite.

Galatians 2:11–14 describes a serious confrontation between Paul and Peter. This incident takes place at Antioch some time before the Jerusalem conference in Acts 15. For Paul, Peter's withdrawal from table fellowship is plainly hypocrisy. He has agreed Gentiles were not converts to Judaism and were fully saved apart from the law. But under pressure from the "men from James," Peter withdraws from fellowship with the Gentiles. For Paul, this is nothing short of a breach of the agreement in the earlier private meeting (Gal 2:1–10).

The Antioch incident has some far-ranging ramifications for Paul. First, it forces the issue of Gentile equality out into the open. No longer will a private meeting do. Paul must now go to Jerusalem to meet publically with all the parties involved (Acts 15). Second, the incident may represent a break between Paul and the Antioch church. He continues his missionary efforts, eventually spending eighteen months in Corinth and three years in Ephesus. By Acts 18, the center of Gentile mission shifts from Antioch to Ephesus. Paul's mission is responsible for planting many churches in the Lycus Valley by the end of the first century. Third, the incident points out what we already know about Paul from Galatians 1—he is not under the authority of the Jerusalem church. Paul was commissioned by the risen Jesus directly and will not tolerate being told to change his gospel by men allegedly from James.

Why does the book of Acts not record the Antioch incident? It is possible Luke thought his inclusion of the Jerusalem conference in Acts 15 was sufficient to summarize the problem of Gentile salvation. Luke tends to emphasize the unity of the church, so the incident at Antioch may have been passed over in order to highlight the unity of the Jerusalem conference.

PAUL CONFRONTS PETER IN ANTIOCH (2:11–14)

The meeting described in Galatians 2:1–10 dealt with the status of Gentiles with respect to Judaism. Paul argued Gentiles are not converting to Judaism and therefore should not be required to be circumcised as a convert to Judaism. The private meeting between Paul and the pillars of the Jerusalem church did not seem to discuss other ramifications of Gentile salvation.

Table Fellowship

The issue in the Antioch incident is Jews and Gentiles sharing table fellowship. This is not simply "eating together." The importance of table fellowship is often underestimated by the modern reader since in the ancient world sharing food with another person made a social statement about yourself and about your guest. For the observant Jew, table fellowship was a complex and important issue since eating with "unclean hands" could render any food unclean.

In the Gospels this theme of separation from the unclean appears frequently. The Pharisees are described as confused by Jesus' association with the "unclean" of their society (Mark 2:15–17; Luke 15:1–2). Jesus regularly shared meals with tax collectors and other "sinners." Jesus understood what it meant socially and theologically to sit down and eat a meal with someone on the fringe of Jewish society. When he chose to eat with someone who was a part of the "underclass," he was crossing a social boundary in order to meet a spiritual need. A Pharisee, on the other hand, would never have ever eaten with a person of unclean status, whether a Jew who was ceremonially unclean or a Gentile, who is by definition unclean.

If those who insist on Gentile circumcision are the same as the "men from James" who insist on separation of Jews and Gentiles at a meal, then it is not implausible they are Pharisees who have accepted Jesus as Messiah and Savior. A Pharisee would never share a meal with Gentile; even a God-fearing Gentile would have been unacceptable (Acts 11:1–3). According to Acts 15:1–2, there are some Pharisees who have accepted Christ and in Acts 21:20 James boasts there are many Jews in the Christian community who are zealous for the law.

It is important to realize the shared meals in the Antioch church were a part of a Christian fellowship and may have included celebrating Communion. Imagine the ramifications of prominent Jewish members of the early church refusing to share in the celebration of the Lord's death and resurrection with other members who were Gentiles. This would imply Gentile believers were in some way less than Christian and not true followers of Jesus. Paul's argument in Galatians is that Gentiles are not secondrate Christians nor do they have lesser status in the body of Christ.

Peter, Barnabas, and Table Fellowship

Peter and Barnabas seem to have had no problem eating with Gentiles prior to a visit from "men from James." Peter would have recalled Jesus' practice of eating with sinners, but even Jesus did not eat with Gentiles. When Peter reluctantly visited the home of the Gentile Cornelius, the Jerusalem community questioned Peter, suspecting he may have eaten with him (Acts 11:3). It is quite possible Peter and Barnabas struggled with participating in table fellowship with Gentiles despite Peter's vision in Acts 10 and his experience with Cornelius.

An additional factor for Peter and Barnabas is Jewish food taboos. Certainly Gentiles would have had no problem with eating meat permitted in the law and it is unlikely any Gentile would consciously offend their Jewish brothers in Christ by serving them pork. But virtually all meat available in a Greco-Roman market would have been sacrificed to a god. This alone would have made the meat unacceptable to a Jew.

The source of meat is not the only issue since it may not be the case every meal shared by the Jewish and Gentile Christians included meat. In the first century, meat was considered an expensive luxury. Christian meals were probably simple meals typical of a Mediterranean city like Antioch. Since Pharisees thought any contact with uncleanliness was enough to result in a state of impurity, even sharing a common cup or loaf of bread with Gentile believers when celebrating Communion could result in ritual impurity. It appears Peter and Barnabas did not object to sharing food with Gentiles until they were questioned by "men from James" (Gal 2:12).

MEN FROM JAMES?

Who are the "men from James"? It is possible these are men sent by James to ensure the churches in Antioch were continuing in the apostolic tradition. Barnabas was sent to Antioch in Acts 11:22–23 for this reason. On the other hand, it is possible these men are not sent by James at all, but merely were part of his circle of disciples and came without James' direct approval. A third possibility is the "men from James" are the same people who are identified as the "Judaizers" in Galatians 1. Most scholars, however, see these as two different groups. The Judaizers are agitators acting outside of the private agreement reached in Galatians 2:1–10 by insisting Gentile converts submit to circumcision. The "men from James" are only concerned with Jewish-Christian practice when sharing a meal. Whatever their relationship with James, they are not there to impose any new commands on the Gentiles. They appear only concerned with the behavior of other Jewish Christians, namely Peter and Barnabas.

First-Century Politics

The political situation in Judea is a major factor in the Antioch incident. Galatians is written about A.D. 50, just as the tensions between Jews and Rome became intense. About A.D. 40 the emperor Caligula demanded the Jews place his statue within the temple itself (*J.W.* 1.10.1–5; *Antiq.* 18:8.2–9; Tacitus, *Hist.* 5.9). Although this command was never carried out and was rescinded after Caligula's death, it contributed to anti-Roman feelings in Judea. When Herod Agrippa I died in A.D. 44 Judea was ruled by increasingly inept Roman procurators. About A.D. 46, Cuspius Fadus took the high-priestly garments into Roman custody in order to prevent the high priest from using his office to foment rebellion. This act had the opposite effect.

About the same time, several "messianic pretenders" and other revolutionary movements developed. Theudas (*Antiq.* 20.5.1) was killed by Fadus (A.D. 44–46) and Tiberius Julius Alexander executed the two sons of Judas the Galilean, James and Simon, sometime in A.D. 46–48 (*Antiq.* 20.6.1). During the rule of Cumanus (A.D. 48–52) there was a riot in Jerusalem which killed twenty to thirty thousand (*Antiq.* 20.5.3; *J.W.* 2.12.1). Josephus says these riots were caused by the Zealots. He goes on to describe the development of "brigands" (*Antiq.* 20.6.1) after these riots.

These are the social bandits or Zealots which lead ultimately to the rebellion against Rome in A.D. 66.

Jews living outside of Judea also dealt with dangerous political situations. There were riots in Alexandria, Egypt, in A.D. 38 primarily because the government began to infringe on Jewish customs (Philo, *In Flaccum* 41–54). Claudius expelled many Jews from Rome in A.D. 41 because of rioting over "Chrestus." In A.D 39–41 there were a number of anti-Jewish riots in Antioch and the rights of the Jews to keep their traditions were under attack. There was therefore a great deal of tension with Rome even for Jews living outside of Judea.

James and Jerusalem

As James Dunn has observed, the Christian Jews living in Jerusalem at the end of the 40s needed to demonstrate they were "good Jews."[1] Perhaps this is the motivation for individuals from Jerusalem to insist Jewish Christians in Antioch keep the traditional boundary markers of circumcision, food laws, and Sabbath. Dunn points out that the followers of Jesus would have still considered themselves Jews and thought of the Jesus movement as a "development and reform" of the Jewish faith.[2] For James, following Jesus as the Messiah is not a new religion at all. Jewish Christianity could be understood as a sect within Judaism, one that believed Jesus was the Messiah and that the messianic age was imminent.

Dunn's second point is less secure. He thinks the authority of the Jerusalem pillars was "generally acknowledged" by all, including Antioch and Paul. It seems to me Paul's argument in Galatians is that his authority is equal to the Jerusalem apostles. After all, he too was called by the resurrected Lord and commissioned to be the apostle to the Gentiles. In matters of Gentile practice, Paul seems to claim primacy. Since the political and social situation of Judea and the Jews in the Diaspora was very difficult, tensions between

---

1. Dunn, "Incident at Antioch," 8.
2. Dunn, "Incident at Antioch," 11.

Jews and Gentiles was strained. The Jewish followers of Jesus found themselves in an extremely hard place: if they continue to practice their faith as Jews, how can they fellowship with Gentiles believers?

PETER'S HYPOCRISY

Paul says Peter's withdrawal from table fellowship with the Gentile is nothing less than hypocrisy. The problem Paul has with Peter is his change of attitude and behavior after the visit from the "men from James." The first verb ("shrink back") is a military term and has the sense of retreating to an "inconspicuous position."[3] In Acts 20:27 Paul uses the verb to describe what he did not do: he did not "shrink back" from preaching the gospel in Ephesus in the face of persecution. The second verb ("separate") has the sense of separating something into groups, as in separating sheep and goats in Matthew 25:32. While this can refer to ritual purity (clean and unclean), there is an eschatological sense here as well. At the end of the age, the Lord will separate those who will enter the kingdom from those who will not. If I am right that the political and religious situation in Judea was becoming increasingly "apocalyptic," it is possible these "men from James" were encouraging a separation of the Jews and the Gentiles in anticipation of the coming judgment.

What Motivated Peter?

The reason for Peter's withdrawal from table fellowship is fear from the "circumcision party," the Jews who insisted on circumcising Gentiles. There is at least the possibility (based on Gal 6:12) some Jews, such as the Zealots, were willing to use force to ensure Jewish traditions were being observed. During the Maccabean period, circumcision of new-born sons was enforced (1 Macc 2:24–26). About 125 B.C. the Hasmonean king of Judea, John Hyrcanus,

---

3. Bauer et al., *Greek-English Lexicon*.

forcibly circumcised an Idumean village in order to "convert" them to Judaism (Josephus, *Antiq.* 13.9.1).

If this is the case, then perhaps Peter is afraid of real persecution by a zealous wing of the Jerusalem church. This is not a case of "The pastor is coming over, hide the beer bottles"! Peter and Barnabas may have withdrawn from fellowship to avoid a potentially violent reprisal from the "zealots" within Jewish Christianity. Paul himself sought to correct what he understood to be a false teaching about the Messiah (Acts 8:1–3). It is impossible to be certain of the source of this persecution but, like pre-Christian Paul, this group was concerned about Diaspora Jewish Christian communities maintaining proper beliefs and practices.

"Shrinking Back"

Peter's actions, then, are out of character. He is not living out his beliefs nor is he keeping the agreement reached with Paul in Galatians 2:1–10. Paul thinks Peter and Barnabas have "shrunk back" out of fear and are therefore in need of correction. While Peter is a hypocrite, Paul describes Barnabas as "led astray." This is a different word which has the sense of being "carried away" by something. Perhaps Barnabas was persuaded by the rhetoric of the "men from James." Barnabas was originally sent to Antioch by Jerusalem and perhaps he was under some additional pressure by these men. His loyalty was to Jerusalem and was associated with the apostolic community since the earliest days (Acts 4). The Gentile mission is Paul's commission; it is not Barnabas's.

All of the Jews in the Antioch church join with Peter and Barnabas in withdrawing from fellowship with the Gentile believers. This indicates there is a church-wide split caused by the "men from James." This is a serious breach of the unity of the church and Paul must confront it as a serious threat to the survival of the work in Antioch.

The Antioch Incident
A PUBLIC CONFRONTATION

Paul publically confronted Peter because his "conduct was not in line with the truth" (Gal 2:14). This confrontation was "before them all," indicating Paul waited until the church assembled to confront Peter. This is in contrast to their first meeting in Jerusalem. Rather than meet privately, Paul chose to bring this issue to the whole assembly in a public setting.

Paul accuses Peter of not living in accordance with what he knows is the truth, based on their previous agreement (Gal 2:1–10). The "men from James," on the other hand, are described with military terms. They are "spies and agitators" who are outside of the truth of the gospel to begin with. While Peter knows the truth and is not acting in accordance with it, the agitators do not even know the gospel.

Paul as an Equal

That Paul would publically confront Peter indicates he sees himself as an equal to Peter, perhaps as a result of the private agreement of Galatians 2:1–10. If Peter and the Jewish Christians withdraw from the Gentile Christians, then there is no unity in the body of Christ. As Paul will point out later in Galatians, there is no Jew or Greek in the body of Christ, we are all members together "in Christ" (Gal 3:28). To separate into two bodies, one Jewish and the other Gentile, misses the point of a "joint body" encompassing all people from every social level (cf. Eph 2:11–22). As Witherington says, "one would have to choose between Jewish purity and body unity. The church cannot have both . . . Paul is arguing that the 'truth of the gospel' is the only real basis for true unity in the Christian church."[4] What is at stake here is the nature of the gospel.

---

4. Witherington, *Grace in Galatia*, 158–59.

The Results of the Confrontation

Did this confrontation have the desired effect? Since the letter does not indicate Peter agreed with Paul and returned to fellowship with the Gentile believers, it would appear Paul's argument was either rejected or at the least left unresolved at the time of the writing of Galatians. If Paul could have claimed Barnabas reversed his actions and rejoined Paul, he would have included the fact as evidence he was correct. The silence about Barnabas in the letter is an indication the matter is still unresolved at that time. Since Peter speaks up for Paul in the Jerusalem conference in Acts 15, it is likely he was moved by Paul's appeal.

Since Barnabas and Paul separate soon after the Jerusalem conference, it may be the wounds of this confrontation were deep. It appears John Mark's return to Jerusalem (Acts 13:13) is a reaction to Paul preaching the gospel to the Roman governor of Cyprus. John Mark may have thought Paul went too far in targeting pagan Gentiles. That Paul and Barnabas separate over John Mark in Acts 15:36–41 may indicate Barnabas is only willing to continue the mission in synagogues to reach God-fearing Gentiles, not in the marketplace to reach pagan Gentiles.

CONCLUSION

For Paul, Peter's withdrawal from table fellowship is not a minor theological difference of opinion. To separate into two groups would destroy the unity of the body of Christ. Paul wants to avoid a situation where Gentiles are not welcome to fellowship and worship with Jews because they do not keep the law, nor does he want to encourage Gentiles to keep the law in order to be a part of the Christian community. As he will make clear in the next section of the letter, all who are in Christ have been crucified with Christ and raised to new life in him. There is therefore no distinction between Jew and Gentile in the body of Christ. Paul's churches in Galatia ought to be places where there is open fellowship across cultural lines because the only thing that matters in the present age is the body of Christ.

This unity of the body of Christ is difficult to apply to modern churches since the church is so divided and fractured. In many cases, denominational divisions are based on important doctrines and practices where unity is impossible. But most Christians have experienced division in churches over issues far from the core of the gospel. Paul encourages the churches in Galatia to maintain the core elements of the gospel as well as to create an open environment where all people (Jew and Gentile, male and female, slave and free) are welcome.

QUESTIONS FOR FURTHER DISCUSSION

1. What do you think really upset Paul about Peter's behavior in Antioch?
2. How can Paul's confrontation of Peter be used as a model for Christians dealing with issues in churches today?
3. How does Paul balance unity within the body of Christ with defending the truth of the gospel?
4. What are some of the main things which divide churches today? Are any of these issues things Paul might consider separating over?

6

Crucified with Christ
Galatians 2:15–21

INTRODUCTION

IN THIS SECTION OF Galatians, Paul concludes the first part of the letter by declaring clearly God has freely justified those who are in Christ by faith and not through works of the law. Since the immediate context is sharing table fellowship with Gentiles (2:11–14) and the larger context of the letter is circumcision of Gentile converts, Paul has in mind the boundary markers which set Jews apart from Gentiles. Some Jewish Christians think Gentiles ought to fully convert to Judaism in order to be right with God, but Paul strongly disagrees. He argues if a person tries to "be right with God" by doing the boundary markers, then they cancel out the grace of God. This is not a difference in opinion over a minor practice but a dangerous rejection of God's clear revelation given to Paul that Gentiles are not required to keep the law.

These verses are a continuation of Paul's response to Peter's withdrawal from table fellowship in 2:11–14, although it is difficult to know where Paul's words to Peter actually end. Certainly 2:14 is presented as direct words to Peter, but it is possible to end Paul's quote at verse 14, after verse 16, after verses 18, or even at the end of the chapter. In any case, we have here the outworking of what Paul said to Peter when he confronted him in Antioch. Paul and Peter no doubt had a lengthy dialogue on the issue, and the discussion could well have included Barnabas and even the "men allegedly from James" who put pressure on the Jews to withdraw from table fellowship in the first place. Galatians 2:15–21 is therefore a short summary of Paul's reasoning for why Peter is being hypocritical by no longer eating with the Gentiles.

JUSTIFIED BY FAITH IN CHRIST (2:15–18)

Paul's main point here is both Jews and Gentiles are saved in the same way; they are "justified by faith." As he will say later in the letter, there is no longer any value to being a Jew or Gentile with respect to salvation since both are saved equally by God's grace.

Jews by Birth, not Sinful Gentiles (2:15–16)

Paul includes himself along with Peter as ethnically Jewish in contrast to the "sinful Gentiles." This is the language of Second Temple-period Judaism. Writers during this period regularly divided the world into Jews (who have the law and a covenant relationship with God) and Gentiles (who by definition do not keep the law). Even among Jewish factions one group might choose to describe another as "sinful" because they exhibit some major difference in practice. For example, Jews who sided with the Greeks in the Maccabean revolt were "sinners" (1 Mac 1:34).

More important for understanding Galatians 2:15, the Pharisees accused Jesus of "eating with sinners" (Mark 2:16). Most of these sinners were followers of Jesus and presumably "repentant sinners," and all of them were Jewish. The Pharisees considered them unclean since they had contact with Gentiles and did not follow the traditions of the Pharisees to avoid eating unclean food. If a Jew could be considered a sinner for having contact with a Gentile, then eating with a Gentile would have been unimaginable for the Pharisees. The "men from James" who convinced Peter and Barnabas to withdraw from table fellowship may have been influenced by the Pharisees. Acts 15:1 alludes to these teachers and in verse 5 there are some "believers who belong to the party of the Pharisees" who state clearly Gentiles must be circumcised and keep the law of Moses.

Paul, Peter, and the men from James are all "Jews by birth," people to whom the law and the covenant was given. They are the ones who are the most blessed by God as opposed to the pagans in Galatia. Yet God has offered salvation to the Gentiles apart from the law and is justifying both Jews and Gentiles.

Yet all Jews know a person is not justified by doing the works of law. In Romans Paul demonstrates all people, whether Jew or Gentile, fall short of the glory of God (Rom 3:23) and therefore stand in need of a Savior. Jews are no different than Gentiles in their need for a gracious God to save them.

WORKS OF THE LAW CAN NEVER JUSTIFY (2:16)

That Jews also rely on the grace of God may come as a surprise for some Christian readers of Galatians who are accustomed to thinking of Judaism as a religion of works. There is a perception among Christians that a Jewish person living at the time of Paul earned their salvation by doing the works of the law and they were in danger of losing their salvation any time they that broke the law. This is an unfortunate misunderstanding of Second Temple Judaism! For the most part, writings from this period indicate Jews were part of the covenant because they were born Jewish and they kept the law to stay in the covenant. Not every Jew was required to be in the state of purity required by the Pharisees.

In fact, most Christians think of the Pharisees as stereotypical legalists who thought they merited salvation for their good works. But by reading the texts popular among Jews in the first century, it does not appear even the Pharisees thought they were earning salvation by means of a "works of the law" merit system.

In fact, this sounds more like the Roman Catholic Church at the time of Luther than Judaism. For most Jews living at the time of Paul, obeying the law was a natural response to God's gracious election of Israel as the covenant people.

But when Paul claims a Gentile can be declared righteous through the faith of Jesus Christ and not by keeping the law, Paul is stepping well beyond the way Jews thought salvation would come to the Gentiles. To be declared righteous before God would have required submission to the law, beginning with the sign of the covenant, circumcision. In addition to circumcision, Gentiles would be expected to keep other key boundary markers like Sabbath and food laws. Paul's insistence Gentiles are saved without obedience to the law means Gentiles are not converting to a form of Judaism, a point he will return to often in Galatians.

What Is Justification?

Justification is a metaphor for salvation drawn from the legal world. In the law, a judge was responsible for hearing a dispute between people and deciding who is innocent or guilty (Deut 25:1). The righteous judge was to give justice to the weak and maintain the rights of the afflicted (Ps 82:3). Since God is the ultimate judge, he decides our innocence or guilt based on our good works on the basis of law, and must find us guilty (Rom 3:23). But for those who have faith in Jesus Christ, Paul says we are "justified," or "declared righteous," by God. Paul regularly says those who are not "in Christ" are under God's condemnation and worthy of punishment.

As a metaphor for salvation, justification is Paul's way of describing the moment of salvation when a person is declared righteous in God's law court. But the sinner who is declared righteous is not actually righteous since all humans still sin even after they are justified. Justification therefore concerns our legal status before God as righteous rather than a present state of personal righteousness.

Galatians

The Basis of Justification

The basis of this declaration is "faith in Jesus" (2:16). The translation of the phrase has been controversial in recent years. Most translations make Jesus the object of our faith by supplying the preposition "in" at the beginning of verse 16. When we believe in Jesus Christ, we are declared righteous by God. But many scholars point out the Greek text should not be translated as "faith in Jesus" but rather the "faith of Jesus." In this understanding, the basis of our justification is the faithfulness of Jesus when he obediently humbled himself to die on the cross. Because of Jesus Christ's faith, we are able to be justified. Jesus is both the faithful one through whom we are justified and the object of our faith as Christians. In the same verse Paul states "we believe in Christ Jesus"; the word "in" does appear in the text and Jesus is certainly the object of our faith.

Although for some this may seem like a hopelessly complicated discussion of the finer points of New Testament Greek, it is important because we want to understand clearly what Paul is saying when he claims we are justified by faith not works of the law. It is the faithful act of Jesus submitting to the humiliation of the cross which enables God to declare us righteous when we place our faith in Jesus and his finished work on the cross.

The "works of righteousness" a person might have done can never merit this declaration, whether it is "works of the law" or some other good deeds as defined by various religious groups throughout church history. People have a natural tendency to want to "work for salvation" or to do good works which "merit salvation." Meriting salvation is at the heart of most religions, and people want to know, "What must I do to be saved?" Paul's answer is simply: believe in the Lord Jesus Christ, the one who has already accomplished salvation in his humble service on the cross.

Why Can't the Law Justify?

Paul is going to return to this issue later in the book, but for now it is important to observe, Paul says, "the works of the law" cannot justify. "The works of the law" refer to the unique practices that separate Jews from the rest of the world, primarily circumcision, food laws, and Sabbath. But as Paul will make clearer in the second section of the book, practice of the boundary markers implies keeping the rest of the law. The works of the law are "particularly those obligations of the law which were reckoned especially crucial in the maintenance of covenant righteousness."[1] Historically speaking, these "works of the law" were used to define Jewish identity prior to the Maccabean Revolt (165 B.C.). When the Seleucid king Antiochus IV Epiphanes specifically outlawed circumcising children, some of the Jews forced parents to obey the law and circumcise their children (Josephus, *Antiq.* 13.9.1).

Contrary to popular belief, the purpose of the law was never to justify people before God. The Old Testament consistently teaches people cannot be righteous before God. In Psalm 143:2 the writer asks God not to judge him since he knows "no one can stand righteously before God." Even though Job maintains his innocence, he admits no one is righteous before God (Job 9:2). The law showed the need for God's grace and provided a system to obtain atonement for sin, but atonement only covered sin until the ultimate ransom for sin, Christ Jesus.

Since Gentile Christians are not converting to Judaism, Paul cannot endorse any teaching which would consider them to be "sinners" under the law again. The opponents are rebuilding the barrier between Jews and Gentiles that was torn down in Christ (Eph 2:14–17).

REBUILDING WHAT IS DESTROYED (2:17–18)

It is important to remember the context of these verses. Paul and Peter were sharing table fellowship with Gentiles believers. Men

---

1. Dunn, *Galatians*, 136.

claiming to be from James arrived and accused them of "eating with sinners." By eating with Gentiles, Peter and Paul were living out justification by faith since there is neither Jew nor Gentile in the body of Christ. But Paul's opponents accuse him of being a sinner, just like the Gentiles. When Peter and Barnabas withdrew from table fellowship, they signaled their agreement with the opponents. Eating with Gentile Christians would cause them to become ceremonially unclean, sinners! The problem in Antioch was not the food on the table, but rather sharing the food with Gentiles who were still impure sinners in the minds of the opponents.

Eating Like Jesus

This accusation against Paul and Peter is similar to the accusation made against Jesus by the Pharisees, who regularly grumbled when Jesus ate with "tax collectors and other sinners" (Luke 15:1–2; Matt 11:19). It is likely some of the sinners with whom Jesus ate were not yet followers. For example, Matthew hosted a meal and invited his friends to eat with Jesus (Matt 9:9–13). To a certain extent, Peter is continuing the kind of ministry Jesus did, treating sinners with grace. But in this case the "sinners" are Gentile Christians who are justified by God and have received the Holy Spirit just as Peter had.

If the Gentile Christians in Antioch have been justified by Christ, then they cannot be regarded as "sinners" any longer. Christ has justified them despite the fact they have not submitted to the law. If Peter is made a "sinner" by eating with the wrong people, then Jesus (who served Peter in John 13 by washing his feet), is a "servant of sinners"! This obviously cannot be the case, but it is the implication of the opponent's claim that eating with Gentiles makes the apostles sinners.

Paul claims anyone who attempts to be justified by works is trying to rebuild something which has already been torn down. This might refer to rebuilding the barrier of the law that was destroyed by Paul's gospel. Since Peter had agreed the Gentile Titus should not be forced to submit to circumcision, Paul understands this breaking of fellowship with Gentiles over food traditions as a step backwards. Peter is redrawing boundaries between Jews and Gentiles which have been destroyed by Jesus (Eph 2:14–18).

Is Christ the Servant of Sin?

Paul asks this rhetorical question to point out the absurdity of his opponent's position. If both Jews and Gentiles are sinners, and both Jews and Gentiles are saved by grace through faith, then it is foolish to consider Christian Gentiles as sinners simply because they do not follow the food laws found in the law.

If the law could not justify, how is it the believer in Christ can be justified before God? For Paul, it is the believer's identification with Christ's death, burial, and resurrection that results in "being right with God." Since Jesus fulfilled the law, our identification with his death, burial, and resurrection means we too have died to the law and been raised to new life in Christ Jesus.

CRUCIFIED WITH CHRIST (2:19–21)

Paul's description of the believer as once dead but now alive in Christ is found in both Romans and Galatians. In Romans 6, however, believers are dead in their sins and are made alive in Christ (6:1–4). Here in Galatians, Paul identifies himself as both "crucified with Christ" as well as "alive in Christ." This paradox is at the heart of his gospel of God's grace.

Dead to the Law, but Alive in Christ (2:19)

How has Paul "died to the law"? It may be Paul has in mind his former life as a Pharisee and his pursuit of righteousness through the law. When he met Christ on the road to Damascus it was as if he died and was raised to a new life in Christ. On the other hand, Paul will show later in the letter the law demonstrates human sinfulness and the need for salvation. Paul may have this in mind here in 2:19. By trying to keep the law all he ending up achieving was showing how far he has fallen short of the glory of God and how deep his need for a Savior really was.

If he has died to law, it is so he can now live to God. This is very similar to Romans 6, where Paul describes his encounter with Jesus as passing from death to life. It is not possible for Paul to reform his old life and be acceptable to God, nor is it possible for him to add belief in Jesus as Messiah to his previous way of thinking and receive justification. Spiritually speaking, Paul needed to die to the law in order to be raised to new life in Christ Jesus.

Crucified with Christ (2:20)

Paul describes the person who has faith in Jesus as totally identified with the death of Jesus. Just as Christ was crucified, so too the believer is dead with respect to sin. The verb is rare and means something like "co-crucified." More importantly, this verb is in the perfect tense in order to highlight the completed work of Jesus. We have (already) been crucified completely and the results of that action continue to resonate in the life of the "living in Christ" believer.

Paul said "I was crucified with Christ" but then "it is not I who lives but Christ." Even though Paul sees himself as dead to sin, it was Christ who was raised to new life and Paul knows he only is alive because Christ lives in him. For Paul, what we are "in Christ" is a wholly new creation (2 Cor 5:20). This new life is available because Jesus "gave himself" for us. The verb Paul chooses here has the nuance of handing over or delivering someone or something (cf. Rom 8:32; 4:25). It is the word used for Judas's betrayal of Jesus, but Paul makes it clear Jesus handed himself over to be crucified. Jesus gave himself for us because he loved us. Paul describes the great love of God several times (1 Thess 1:4; 2 Thess 2:16). As F. F. Bruce said, "it was a source of unending wonder to him 'that I, even I, have mercy found."[2]

The implication is that our "resurrection with Jesus" is our new life and this new life is not at all like the old one. Jesus now

---

2. Bruce, *Galatians*, 146.

lives through us. This new life has several implications. First, the life we live now is not our own life but Jesus living in and through us. A person who is in Christ cannot claim to have contributed to their salvation in any way.

Second, if the person who is in Christ has been raised to new life, they ought to live that new life. If a child refuses to eat or drink, the child will not grow properly and become sick. Parents would take the child to a doctor and try to discover why their child was not doing what a child naturally does. In a similar way, it is "natural" for a child of God to develop spiritually. The one who is in Christ needs to behave in ways which promote spiritual growth and development as a child of God.

Third, for Paul this new life implies the old life has been crucified. The immediate application in Galatians is the law, and he will reinforce this point in chapters 3-4. But everyone who is in Christ has died to their old life. To return to aspects of the old life which were not healthy for the new life is dangerous. Part of growing in Christ is understanding what things are really important for the new life we have through Christ.

Paul's opponents in his Galatian churches were placing their identification with Jesus at risk by demanding Gentiles convert to Judaism and keep the law. Not only are they rebuilding barriers that have been torn town, they are in danger of nullifying the grace of God.

NULLIFYING THE GRACE OF GOD (2:21)

Paul says Christians who try to keep the law "nullify the grace of God" (2:21). The verb "nullify" refers to not recognizing something as valid. This might happen in two ways. First, a person might come to faith in Christ and be "dead to the law and alive in Christ" but then not live in the freedom they have in Christ. There are some Christians who try to keep aspects of the law such as Sabbath or food laws, or redefine elements of the law and impose them as markers of real Christian faith. For example, describing baptism as the replacement for circumcision as a "sign of the covenant" seems to miss the point Paul is making in Galatians 2 and is effectively "rebuilding what has been torn down." Many Christian communities create boundaries to define their group in contrast to others. Some of these may be valid (such as doctrinal differences), but other boundaries take the form of implicit definitions of a "real Christian." These assumed community values are really legalistic rules and are similar to being "dead to the law" yet attempting to still keep it.

A second, opposite response to being dead to the law is to fully embrace freedom in Christ and "sin that grace may abound." While this seems to be a common attitude in modern Christianity, there has always been a problem with Christians who rightly believed they were fully saved and could not lose their salvation but wrongly believed they could behave any way they liked. The early church struggled with people who took their freedom from the law to mean they had no moral restraints at all. The letter of Jude, for example, is written to defend the faith against those who have secretly slipped into the church to "pervert the grace of God into a license for sin and immorality" (Jude 4).

These two ways of nullifying God's grace were problems in Paul's churches. He guards against both extremes in both Galatians and Romans. Legalists are a problem in Philippi and the Corinthian church seemed to struggle with their freedom. Here in Galatians Paul is attacked by Jewish Christians insisting the law is required in order to encourage moral behavior among the Gentiles. Indeed, it is likely some Gentile believers needed ethical correction.

Paul concludes by declaring if righteousness could come from the law, then the death of Christ was unnecessary (2:21). Because the law could not justify, God graciously sent his Son to fulfill the law and offer justification by faith.

CONCLUSION

Paul has argued throughout the first two chapters of Galatians the gospel of grace he preached to the churches is the same gospel he received directly from God. Paul says he was called to be an apostle by the resurrected Lord Jesus and was given a commission to preach the gospel to the Gentiles. Just as with the preaching of the Twelve, the content of Paul's gospel is the crucifixion and resurrection of Jesus. But he is adamant that Gentiles are not converting to a form of Judaism and they are therefore not expected to keep the Jewish law. Some Jewish Christians had a problem with this teaching and appear to have argued against Paul in his own churches.

This is such an important point for Paul he was willing to confront Peter and Barnabas directly when they appeared to be hypocritical by not eating with Gentile Christians. The Antioch incident shows Paul's independence from the Twelve as well as his tenacious defense of God's grace, even if it created a rift between himself and a long-time supporting church at Antioch.

The letter of Galatians is about accepting the grace God has given. This is not as easy as it sounds because, like the Galatians believers, we have trouble accepting a completely free gift. There must be a catch, some hidden expectation we were not expecting. As a result, we try to "pay God back" for his free gift by doing good works we think will merit grace. On the other hand, some will abuse freedom in Christ and act any way they like. For Paul, both of these extremes miss the point of the gospel and rob the grace of God of its power.

QUESTIONS FOR FURTHER DISCUSSION

1. What are some things Christians do in order to "merit" salvation? These might be rituals or traditions which are commonly practiced.

2. What are some practical ways Christians can live out a life that has been "crucified with Christ"?

3. In your experience, which is more common, legalism or abuse of freedom? Why do you think this is the case?

7

Law and Faith
Galatians 3:1–12

INTRODUCTION

THE FIRST TWO CHAPTERS of Galatians deal with the relationship of Paul and the Jerusalem church. In those chapters Paul claimed he was commissioned directly by God to preach his gospel to the Gentiles (1:1–2, 11–12) and that he is not under the authority of the apostles in Jerusalem (1:13–24). In fact, he consulted Jerusalem only when his success among the Gentiles raised the question of circumcision of converts (2:1–10). The pillars of the church at Jerusalem agreed with Paul that Titus, a representative test case, should not be circumcised. Later, Paul was forced to publically confront Peter for withdrawing from table fellowship with Gentiles. Paul is clearly independent of the Jerusalem church.

Beginning in chapter 3, Paul begins an argument from Scripture to demonstrate that God is doing something new in the present age. While the prophets of the Hebrew Bible often foresaw the salvation of the Gentiles, their eventual salvation was always through Israel. In the present age, however, Gentiles are able to be right with God without becoming part of the nation of Israel or by doing the "works of the law." This is Paul's main contribution to

Christian theology and something he has already called a "revelation from God" (Gal 1:11-12). In Ephesians 3:1-6 Paul calls this revelation a mystery not revealed to anyone until God made it known to him.

In order to prove this point, Paul must first deal with the purpose of the law. Is it possible a person could keep the law and be declared righteous by God? If that is not the case, why was the law given in the first place?

THE LAW CANNOT MAKE ONE RIGHTEOUS

This is a very dense section of the letter. Paul alludes to or quotes several texts from the Hebrew Bible to make his point that the law did not make a person righteous. In fact, Paul says those who live under law are "under a curse." Using the story of Abraham, Paul argues it is only through faith one can be counted as righteous. Paul packs together several texts from the Hebrew Bible in order to explain the issue and he requires a great deal from his readers. They need to know not only what these verses say, but also the context in which these verses originally appear.

Why Abraham?

That Abraham "believed in God and was declared righteous" is an important point for Paul. But it is critical to Paul's point to know *when* Abraham believed. He trusted in God's word before the sign of the covenant was given, in Genesis 15 not 17. What is more, Abraham believed in God well before his great demonstration of faith in Genesis 22. The reader needs to know the whole flow of the Abraham story in Genesis 12-24 in order to grasp the full impact of Paul's point.

Paul also uses Abraham as an example in both Romans and Galatians. Why select Abraham as the model of faith? It is possible the agitators themselves have been using Abraham in their teaching. But the experience of the Galatian believers is not unlike that of Abraham, who believed and "it was credited to him as righteousness" (Gal 3:7-9).

Paul is creating a biblical argument focusing on the phrase "credited as righteousness" in Genesis 15. In this story, Abraham believed in the word of God as revealed to him and God considered him "right with God" as a result. At this point in history, Abraham should be considered a Gentile, at least by the rules imposed by the agitators in the Galatian churches. He was uncircumcised and the food and Sabbath laws had not yet been given. Since he believed in the God who called him out of his father's land, he was a "converted pagan," just like the Galatian believers.

This is in contrast to other views of Abraham in the Judaism of the Second Temple period. For example, in the apocryphal book Sirach, Abraham is described as having kept the "law of the Most High," so God entered into a covenant with him and "certified the covenant in his flesh" (Sir 44:19-21). Paul does not rewrite Scripture like so much of the literature of the Second Temple period did. He considers Abraham as a Gentile who was made right with God by faith in what God told him, not by works (either circumcision or the law). Abraham is therefore the perfect model for Paul to use since he was justified before the law: he was justified by faith not by the act of circumcision.

Habakkuk in Context

Paul quotes Habakkuk 2:4 in Galatians 3:11 in order to call to mind a series of important events. The prophet Habakkuk lived just prior to the fall of Jerusalem and was concerned about the great injustice of the evil empire of Babylon being used by God to punish Judah. It does not seem right to Habakkuk a just and righteous God would allow Babylon to exist, much less use it to execute judgment on his covenant people. The prophet expresses the exilic struggle to understand how the Jewish people could continue to be God's people after being punished by a long exile.

In response to Habakkuk's complaints, God tells the prophet both the fall of Jerusalem and the exile are a result of covenant unfaithfulness. Israel has fallen under the "curse of the law" as described in Deuteronomy. The righteous, however, must live by faith. To say those under the law are "under a curse" requires more than the single line from Deuteronomy cited by Paul. His argument is therefore based on a whole theology of "curse and blessing" in the law.

Paul's Use of Scripture

The density of this argument requires so much from the reader it is hard to know exactly who Paul is addressing in the Galatian churches. If Paul is addressing pagan converts to Christianity, would they appreciate the rhetorical impact of this scriptural argument? But based on Paul's speeches before pagan audiences in Acts 14 and 17, it appears Paul would not have made an argument based on Scripture to a recently-converted-from-paganism congregation. 1 Thessalonians was written to a congregation who had recently "turned from idols" and has very little reference to the Old Testament.

Alternatively, two possibilities remain to explain Paul's target of scriptural argument in Galatians 3, although they are not mutually exclusive. First, Paul could be addressing God-fearing Gentiles. These are people who were already practicing a form of Judaism before hearing Paul's gospel and were now being advised to fully convert to Judaism in order to be right with God. They had sufficient experience hearing how the Old Testament was read in the synagogue and they would have been prepared to appreciate Paul's point.

Second, Paul may be using these particular verses because they are the texts used by the agitators. If Abraham was being presented as a prototypical Gentile convert to Judaism, then perhaps Paul's opponents could be arguing the sign of the covenant with Abraham was circumcision. For the agitators, a present-day Gentile should be like Abraham and fully convert to Abraham's faith.

GALATIANS

FOOLISH GALATIANS! (3:1-9)

Paul begins with a stinging bit of rhetoric: "Who has bewitched you?" (3:1) Twice in the first three verses of this chapter Paul calls the Galatians "foolish." This does not mean they are ignorant and need to be taught what is right. They have already received the gospel and they know the truth, but they are deliberately choosing to behave in a way which does not line up with the truth.

Foolish or Bewitched?

It is also possible to describe foolishness in the Greco-Roman world as going beyond moral failure to a lack of respect for social boundaries. When a person crossed social boundaries they behaved foolishly and risked shaming themselves. Paul therefore calls the Galatians foolish since they clearly know how they ought to be living but are choosing to live in a way which is not in accordance with the truth. In so doing they prove they are foolish and are open to shaming themselves.

But Paul seems to go further than this. The Galatian believers are acting like they have been bewitched. Literally this word means to fall under an "evil eye." In the ancient world it was common for people to believe someone could look at you just the right way and put a "curse" on you. The "evil eye" was well-known in both the Jewish and Hellenistic worlds and there are many magical texts describing how to avoid an evil eye or get rid of such a curse. Since the Galatians are converts from paganism, the implication they are acting like someone "put them under a spell" would have rhetorical impact.

While it is possible Paul thinks the agitators have literally "cast a spell" on the Galatians, it is better to see this as a metaphor. The Galatians are acting like someone has cursed them. They have become "bewitched" by the rhetoric of the agitators. When one is under a spell, they do not think clearly and they do the bidding of a person who is controlling them. That is how the Galatians are behaving at this moment; they have come under the influence of a persuasive teacher who has convinced them to abandon the gospel they originally knew to be true for some sort of false gospel.

If the Gentiles in the Galatian churches think they ought to keep the law, they are not thinking clearly. Paul says they are muddled in their minds, so he appeals to their experience as well as Scripture to convince them they are not under the law. In fact, they are better off if they are not under the law!

HOW DID YOU GET THE SPIRIT?

Paul begins with a logical inference based on the experience of Galatians churches (3:2–6). He asks them, "How did you receive the Spirit?" That the Galatian churches experienced the Spirit is clear from these verses, but Paul does not explain how they experienced the Spirit. It is usually assumed Paul refers to miracles or some ecstatic experience, and verse 5 implies the Galatians had witnessed miracles.

But Paul may not have only miracles in mind. In 1 Thessalonians 1:5–6 Paul says the church came to Christ because of the Holy Spirit. It is possible Paul did some miracles in Thessalonica, but they are not recorded in Acts 17:1–9. Paul's preaching was persuasive in Thessalonica because the Holy Spirit moved in the hearts of people. It was the Holy Spirit who washes the believer and gives the believer new life in Christ (Titus 3:5–6). Here in Galatians, Paul wants to remind the readers how the Holy Spirit moved in their hearts at the moment they believed.

What Makes You Right with God

The Galatian believers are asked to recall how it was they first experienced the gospel of Jesus Christ. They did not experience salvation because they kept the law, but rather because the Holy Spirit did something in their hearts. If Paul is writing to pagan converts, then there is no question about keeping God's law, because they never had. If the Galatian believers were God-fearing

Gentiles, then they know they did not fully convert to Judaism nor did they fully keep the law. In either case, the Galatians must conclude they received the Spirit by God's grace through faith, not through works of the law.

This is an excellent point to make when one struggles with legalism. Did we come to faith in Christ by keeping a series of rules imposed by a church or a human teacher? Did God require us to make changes in our lives before we were "good enough" to be saved? It is the Spirit of God who enables us to express faith, and no "good deed," ritual, or personal holiness is required. In fact, the more personal holiness one has the less likely they will be to accept the free gift of salvation, since they do not think they need salvation.

The Spirit and the New Covenant

In the Old Testament, the Spirit of God was associated with the beginning of the new covenant. For example, in Jeremiah 31:31–33 there will be a time at some point in the prophet's future when God will make a new covenant with his people and he will enable them to keep this new covenant. This enablement comes through the Spirit of God. In Ezekiel 18:31 this new ability to keep God's law is called a "new heart" which replaces the old "heart of stone."

At the Last Supper, Jesus describes his death as initiating the new covenant (Luke 22:20; 1 Cor 11:25). If Jesus death and resurrection is the sacrifice which is associated with the beginning of the new covenant, then the coming of the Holy Spirit would have been expected. Jesus tells his followers to wait in Jerusalem for the Holy Spirit (Acts 1:4–5). In Acts 2 the disciples experience the Holy Spirit for the first time and recognized that this outpouring of the Holy Spirit fulfills prophecies of the messianic age (Acts 2:16–21, quoting Joel 2:28–32).

The Holy Spirit is therefore the sign of the new covenant, not the act of circumcision. If a Gentile convert has received the Holy Spirit, then they have been made right with God and are participating in the new covenant.

WORKS OF THE LAW

Paul contrasts the Spirit with the "works of the law" (3:5-6). What does he have in mind with this phrase? Since the main issues in Galatians 2 were circumcision and food traditions, some scholars suggest the "works of the law" in 3:5-6 does not refer to the whole law. The "works of the law" are the particular boundary markers which set the Jews apart as Jews. If one was not a monotheist, circumcised, and keeping the food traditions and Sabbath, then they were "not a Jew." It is possible Paul has in mind these so-called boundary markers since these would be the first practices the agitators would have insisted Gentiles adopt. If the Galatian churches had a high percentage of God-fearing Gentiles, they might already be keeping Sabbath and food laws.

Since the letter concerns adopting circumcision as a sign of the covenant, it is possible some of Paul's converts were adopting other boundary markers. But Paul's point in Galatians is one that cannot accept part of the law without accepting the whole law. The Galatians are not free to pick and choose which laws they want to keep. If they adopt the boundary markers, they are required to keep the whole law.

The Holy Spirit is of primary importance for Paul in Galatians. It is the Spirit which indicates the Galatian believers are in fact justified and "made right" with God. Later in the letter Paul says it is by the Holy Spirit believers are adopted into the family of God (4:4-6). Since the Spirit was active in their lives before they decided to do the works of the law, Paul concludes the works of the law have nothing to do with being right with God.

ABRAHAM BELIEVED

The experience of the Galatian believers is not unlike that of Abraham, who believed and "it was credited to him as righteousness" (3:7-9). Paul turns to a biblical argument focusing on the phrase "credited as righteousness" in Genesis 15. In this story, Abraham believed in the word of God as revealed to him and God considered him "right with God" as a result.

When Was Abraham Justified?

How did "scripture foresee that God would justify the Gentiles by faith" (3:3, 8)? The Abrahamic covenant states the whole world would be blessed by the seed of Abraham (Gen 12:1–3). Exactly how the nations would be blessed is left unstated, but we know from Galatians it is through the death and resurrection of Jesus the nations are able to participate in the blessing of Abraham's covenant.

While it is possible there were Jews living at the time of Paul who would have disagreed at this point, most would have agreed God would do something in the future to bring the Gentiles into his kingdom. The only disagreement was on how the nations would respond when the Messiah comes. But no Jewish group in the first century would have expected God to justify the Gentiles by faith apart from the "works of the law."

The fact Gentiles would be blessed by the seed of Abraham should not be a surprise to the Jewish church. There are many Old Testament texts which describe Gentiles coming to Jerusalem or Mount Zion to worship the Lord (Isa 2:3–4; 25:6–8; Zech 14:16). What was a shock to the Jewish Christians is that Gentiles were being justified apart from the law. This was unanticipated in the Old Testament. This was a radical idea which offended many conservative Jews, as can be seen by the often violent reaction to Paul's gospel.

Paul's argument, therefore, is that Abraham was declared righteous before the rite of circumcision and the law. Abraham therefore becomes the model for the Gentiles since he too was a Gentile, saved by faith in God and not by works of the law. In fact, the law will never result in faith since those who are under the law are "under the curse of the law."

THE LAW BRINGS CURSE; FAITH BRINGS LIFE (3:10-14)

Paul quotes the book of Deuteronomy to argue that the one who tries to do the whole law finds themselves under the curse of the law. The law itself promised the one who lived in accordance with the law would be blessed but the one who did not live according to the law would be under a curse. Is Paul talking only about the works of the law, the boundary marker issues which the agitators are trying to impose on the Galatians? Probably not, since it is the whole law that was in view in the original "blessing and cursing" passage. If one does the "boundary markers," one is obligated to do the whole law.

Paul will return to this later in the letter, but here he states the law never could make one right with God because it was always impossible to keep the whole law. God anticipated his people's inability to be completely holy by giving them the sacrificial system. Whenever there was a transgression of law, sacrifice could be made. In fact, many of the things in the law which required sacrifices are not sins but rather breaches of cleanliness (Lev 13-15, for example). Ultimately the law pointed out the need for atonement for sin through a sacrifice and defined how a person ought to live.

THE RIGHTEOUS WILL LIVE BY FAITH

The problem is the law could not empower a person to actually live out the law perfectly. The one who has received the Spirit is empowered to live righteously. On the other hand, Paul quotes Habakkuk 2:4 in Galatians 3:11 in order to show that the one who lives by faith is right with God. The context of Habakkuk is the fall of Jerusalem and the beginning of the exile. Habakkuk lived when Israel and Judah were experiencing the ultimate curse of the law, exile from the land promised to Abraham.

The Curse of the Law

Paul declares the death and resurrection of Jesus dealt with the curse of the law, allowing Gentiles to come to be justified through the Spirit, apart from the law. Paul states "Christ redeemed us" from the curse of the law. Paul's use of "Christ" is significant since this is the Messiah. The mission of the Messiah was to redeem his people from the curse of the law. How was this done? The Jewish people had broken the law repeatedly and gone into exile as a result of the curse of the law. The Jewish people in the first century were still under foreign domination. They were still in exile in a very real sense but also in a spiritual sense because they continue to "fall short of the glory of God." Because Israel is under the curse of the law, they too are in need of redemption.

It is as if Israel was in Egypt again, awaiting a decisive act of God to bring them out of their slavery. In the Old Testament their rescue from Egypt was described as "redemption." In Isaiah 40–55 the redemption of God's people from exile in Babylon is described as a "second exodus." But the ultimate decisive act of God which brings about a real redemption from slavery is the death and resurrection of Jesus, the Messiah. The role of the Messiah was not to conquer enemies and thereby bring about the redemption of Israel, but rather to suffer the curse of the law, be hung on a tree, and therefore become the curse for Israel.

CONCLUSION

In this section of Galatians Paul looks at the whole story of the Old Testament in order to demonstrate to his Gentile readers they are made right with God apart from the law, just as Abraham was in Genesis 15. If the Gentiles in Galatia think they can keep the law, they are fooling themselves since they have already been justified by God through faith as evidenced by the Holy Spirit. It is impossible to go back again to the old covenant since it has been fulfilled in the faith work of Jesus on the cross.

It is important for Christians today to see where they live in the history of redemption. Because we live in an age which is not governed by the old covenant and the law, it is foolish to try and go back to law in order to be right with God.

QUESTIONS FOR FURTHER DISCUSSION

1. What is the role of the Old Testament law for the believer today?
2. Are there some commands in the law which can be described as "principles of God" and are therefore applicable in every age? What are some examples of these? How can someone know which commands are principles of God and which are not?
3. Even if we are not to keep the law, can we use the law as a model for ethical and moral decisions today? What are some examples of this?

8

Law and Promise

Galatians 3:13–22

INTRODUCTION

SINCE I AM A university professor, I am familiar with "graduation requirements." Students need to complete lists of tasks in order to pass classes. They need to pass the right number of classes with minimum grades in order to graduate. Usually there are other graduation requirements in addition to classes (pay off your bill, return your library books, pay the graduation fees, attend the graduation ceremony, etc.) These are all tangible items which can be checked off a list. Students know they are close to graduation because their list of completed tasks is growing.

Beginning in Galatians 3, Paul began to argue from Scripture that God is doing something new in his gospel. The "tangible list" from the previous age is no longer appropriate. Even though the prophets foresaw the salvation of the Gentiles, they never anticipated God would save Gentiles apart from the law. Paul describes this new understanding of Gentiles and the law as a "revelation from God" (Gal 1:11–12). In the first part of Galatians 3 Paul began with the spiritual experience of the Galatians themselves: they received the Spirit before they tried to obey the law. He then moved to the scriptural argument based on the faith of Abraham in Genesis 15.

In the second part of this argument Paul reflects on the promise made to Abraham as a legal contract, a testament or will. God promised he would bless the whole world through the seed of Abraham. Because God is a faithful covenant partner, he will certainly keep his promise. But the descendants of Abraham (Israel) were unfaithful and did not keep their part of the covenant. They were unable or unwilling to "bless the whole world" and as a result they fell under the curse of the law. Ultimately they were sent into exile in Assyria and Babylon. This exile continues into Paul's time since the Jews were still scattered throughout the whole world. But God always intended to keep his promise despite the failure of his people. Therefore God will bless the whole world through the ultimate seed of Abraham, Jesus the Messiah.

AN ANALOGY: A COVENANT CANNOT BE SET ASIDE (3:13-18)

Beginning in verse 13, Paul's point is to prove Gentiles receive the promised Spirit through faith, like Abraham, and not through law. The Holy Spirit is associated with the new covenant, so the agitators in the Galatian churches may have been teaching people they cannot receive the Spirit unless they were participants in the old, Mosaic covenant. This means keeping the law, beginning with the circumcision, food, and Sabbath laws. There is a certain logic to this: the new covenant was supposed to enable God's people to keep God's law by writing it on their hearts.

Paul introduces an analogy which would have been familiar to his readers. Since the promise made to Abraham was a covenant promising an inheritance, the analogy of a testament or will is appropriate. Witherington suggests this should be read as "a human will or testament that was irrevocable, like the covenant set up by God."[1] Whatever the background, Paul's main point in this

---

1. Witherington, *Grace in Galatia*, 243.

analogy is the original testament cannot be set aside by a later testament, nor can it be legally modified by an additional codicil. Since the Abrahamic covenant and the Mosaic covenant are separate covenants, Paul says one cannot change the other. There may be similarities, but the law cannot cancel the promise.

WHAT IS A COVENANT?

It is important to understand what a covenant is in this context. A covenant is not a treaty between two equal partners, but rather a unilateral arrangement made by a superior person. God is not "making a deal" with Abraham, promising to bless Abraham only if he keeps his side of the bargain. God simply says, "This is what I am going to do for you." Perhaps it is better to think of this covenant like a grant with no strings attached.

Covenant as a Gracious Gift

In the case of the promise to Abraham, the covenant is God's gracious promise to give Abraham a family, a land, and a special relationship between God and his people. Genesis 12:1–3 is a declaration of what God intends to do, rather than a contract between Abraham and God. The promise to Abraham was a gracious gift given by God and a unilateral covenant since only God made the covenant. As such, this covenant is irrevocable. God's character guarantees the promise made to Abraham will result in a blessing for the whole world.

If God has made a promise to Abraham, he will certainly fulfill his promise. If the law did not cancel the promise, and the promise is being fulfilled by Gentiles coming to Christ in faith, then it is possible to describe the law as a parenthesis between the promise and the fulfillment in the present age.[2] This anticipates several of the analogies Paul will use in his explanation of the purpose of the

---

2. Bruce, *Galatians*, 154.

law. In Galatians 3:24–25, for example, Paul describes the law as a tutor; when maturity comes the tutor is no longer necessary.

Jesus as the Son of Abraham

How God fulfills that promise, according to Paul, is through Jesus Christ. He is the "offspring" originally promised in Genesis 12. This might seem like an unusual reading of the promise to Abraham, but there is some ambiguity in the original story. The "offspring" was to be a "great nation," but the main threat to God's promise is Abraham's childlessness. Abraham has no offspring in Genesis 12 and it is impossible for Sarai to have a child.

Yet the great nation promise must start with Abraham having a child. Paul is exploiting this ambiguity in the original story to point to Jesus as the ultimate son of Abraham. More than this, Paul argues all those who are in Christ are Abraham's offspring as well. The "offspring" is both singular (Jesus) and plural (all those who have faith). By faith in Christ a person in the present age becomes an heir of Abraham, as witnessed by the activity of the Holy Spirit (3:14).

THE ATTRACTION OF THE LAW

Why would someone submit to the law at this point in salvation history if keeping the law is neither necessary nor beneficial? First, people wanted to keep the law out of a sincere desire to serve God correctly. There have been several popular books written by people who tried to keep all of the commands of the Bible, including the Old Testament law. While some are intended to mock the law, these sorts of books raise an important question: If God commanded something in the law, should we not at least try to obey the command?

Paul's answer in Galatians 3 is to understand the context of the command. God told Noah to build an ark, but no one thinks this applies to them (at least they do not begin to build a boat in their backyard to survive a coming flood). They understood the command applied to a particular time and place. Paul is not telling the Galatian churches to just obey God no matter what, but to understand what it is God wants from them at this particular time and place in salvation history.

Who Is In? Who Is Out?

Second, since the Galatians were being told to keep the "boundary markers," it is at least possible the attraction for members of the new community of believers was to define boundaries so one could know who was "in" the church and who was "out." The Jewish boundary markers worked well to define Jews as a separate people, so perhaps some Gentile Christians wanted to adopt these boundary markers in order to demonstrate they are "in Christ."

Marking boundaries is very important to humans. When Jesus said the second greatest commandment is to love one's neighbor, he was immediately asked exactly who counted as a neighbor (Luke 10:25–29). People always want to know the limits of a command. When a child is offered a cookie, the first question is usually "how many?" If there were no rule, some kids would grab as many cookies as their hands could hold. Parents naturally set boundaries for their children for their own good.

The Gentile Christians in Galatia may have simply wanted a tangible list of things they could "do" in order to demonstrate they were part of the body of Christ. Paul's gospel makes it clear works do not make you saved nor will they keep you saved. Your identity as a child of God is what counts. But "be a child of God" is very difficult to comprehend without a set of rules defining what a child of God does or does not do!

Keeping People Out

Third, boundaries exclude as much as they include. Maybe people are attracted to legalism not because it makes them appear to be insiders but so they can exclude other people who do not conform to their view of what a Christian should be. If someone does not behave quite the way I define a Christian, I can consider them an "outsider" and I do not have to treat them like a brother in Christ any longer. One of the real problems with Paul's view of "freedom in Christ" is that people do not like to be free. We want the boundaries and rules, so we create more intense rules and regulations in order to separate ourselves out as spiritual. Paul would likely have a few choice words for modern Galatians!

If this is a correct understanding of the promise to Abraham, then the obvious question is, "What is the purpose of the law?" Paul anticipates this question in 3:19–20.

WHAT WAS THE PURPOSE OF THE LAW? (3:19–20)

These two verses are incredibly important and are critical for a proper understanding of Paul. In fact, how one reads these two verses says a lot about how they are going to understand the rest of Paul's theology. For some scholars, there is a difference between these verses and the book of Romans. It appears as though Paul has a negative attitude toward the law in Galatians but a positive one in Romans (Rom 9:4–5). The modern reader of Galatians and Romans must remember Paul was a Jew and understood the law as God's revelation to the people of Israel. Paul is rightly upset about misuse of the law in the Galatian churches, but in Romans he is describing the perfection of the law in order to highlight what God has done through Jesus Christ.

Because of Transgression

According to Galatians 3:19–20, the law was "added because of transgression until the offspring should come." This verse is remarkable because Paul says the law had both a beginning as well as an end point. Almost every Jew in the first century would have said the law is eternal and there would be no time in history when the law is no longer necessary. For example, Josephus said "... for amongst most other nations it is a studied art how men may transgress their laws; but no such thing is permitted amongst us; for though we be deprived of our wealth, of our cities, or of other advantages we have, our law continues immortal" (*Against Apion* 2.277). In *Jubilees* 3:31, a book written about 150 B.C., it is said Adam and Eve ought to cover their shame because "it is prescribed on the heavenly tablets as touching all those who know the judgment of the law."

Some have sought to deal with Paul's belief that law would end by making a distinction between the ceremonial laws (sacrifices, rituals, food laws, etc.) and the moral laws (the Ten Commandments). This is attractive since it allows the modern Christian to use the law to deal with contemporary social issues. But in Galatians 3:19–20 Paul does not claim some parts of the law have ceased while others continue to be in effect. Paul says the whole law was temporary since it was for the time between the giving of the covenant to Moses and the ultimate fulfillment of the covenant in Jesus Christ.

It is not at all remarkable that Paul sees the history of salvation as a series of periods; from Abraham until the law, then from the law until Christ. Describing salvation history as a series of periods is not unusual for Paul or in first-century Judaism. Paul refers to "this present evil age" in contrast with "the age to come" (Eph 1:21). In this particular case the periodization of salvation history marks off the beginning and end of the law.

The Law Makes Us Aware of Sin

When Paul says the reason the law was given was "transgression," what does this mean? Transgression means a breach of law, specifically the Mosaic law. This is opposed to sin, since one can break a law without being morally deficient (bodily changes, mold on a tent wall, etc.) Following N. T. Wright, the law was added to turn sin, which already existed, into a transgression of the law.[3] This makes humans aware of the moral aspect of sin as well as the legal offense against God. C. K. Barrett says something similar: "Its effect was . . . to make sin everywhere observable in the form of transgression."[4] The law identifies what aspects of life are offensive to the holiness of God, but it allows for an atonement to be made when people break the law.

Law Can Encourage Sin

Unfortunately, a perfectly good law can become a "stimulus to sin." In Romans 7:14–25, Paul says he would not have known sin unless the law told him not to sin. When the law forbids something, humans are prone by nature to break that law. Ultimately the law shows how far short of the glory of God we really are—there is virtually no aspect of our lives which can be described as "holy" and acceptable to God. Every aspect of life is in need of redemption. The law, therefore, stands "in-between" the promise made to Abraham and the fulfillment of the promise in Jesus.

The law was added until the ultimate "seed of Abraham" comes. Paul plays on an ambiguity in the promise itself. The word translated as "offspring" or "seed" is a collective noun and can refer to an individual or a group. Abraham was promised "offspring." Does that refer to a single child (Isaac) or a nation (Israel)? For Paul, the ultimate offspring of Abraham is Jesus, the Messiah. He is the only one of Abraham's children who can be described as a blessing to the whole world. Later in Galatians Paul will extend this metaphor to include all who believe as the children of Abraham (3:29).

---

3. Wright, *Climax of the Covenant*, 160–61.
4. Barrett, *Freedom and Obligation*, 50.

GALATIANS

IS THE LAW OPPOSED TO THE PROMISE OF GOD? (3:21-22)

Another potential problem with Paul's statement that the law was added "because of transgression" is the law could be seen negatively, something opposed to the good promise of God. Paul objects to this strongly. The "certainly not" in 3:21 is the strongest possible contradiction in Greek. The law was a positive part of God's plan to redeem the world, but the law was a step in God's plan which is now in the past.

The Law Cannot Make Alive

Paul states clearly the law cannot impart life (3:21). It "imprisoned everything under sin." Paul's point is the law was not designed to help people obtain righteousness. Most Christians think if the Jews were to be able to keep the law they would be considered righteous and "saved." According to Paul, this was never the purpose of the law. It was given to demonstrate the need for a gracious Redeemer. In the law there was ample provision for sacrifice to cover sin, but also provision to cover other aspects of holiness such as ritual uncleanliness.

Even in the Old Testament God's people believed that if sacrifices covered sin, then moral behavior did not matter. This is especially clear in the prophets, who routinely condemned Israel for making proper sacrifices with a wicked and corrupt heart. In Amos 5:21-24 God tells Israel he despises their worship and festivals because they do not practice the justice at the heart of the law. In Hosea 6:6 God states he does not desire sacrifice, but rather mercy. According to the prophets, the perfect practice of religion will never overcome a lack of justice and mercy.

Obtaining Righteousness through the Law

Would it be possible for a person to obtain righteousness if they came as close to perfection as possible and then made the appropriate sacrifices? Again, this was not the purpose of the law in the first place. The sacrifices were not "extra credit" before God, somehow making up for a lack of righteousness. It is not a case of "do your best and let the sacrifices take care of the rest." What made a person "right with God" under the law was the belief God's grace would cover a person's sin. Psalm 51:17 says God is not pleased with sacrifice, but rather with a "broken and contrite heart." This idea is also found also in Samuel's condemnation of King Saul after the king attempted to make a sacrifice to cover his sin (1 Sam 15:22–23). Paul's point here in Galatians is consistent with the Old Testament: no one ever could obtain righteousness by the law because this was never the function of the law.

Yet the law did promise life to the one who would keep it (Lev 18:5). But to the one who would not keep it, the law was a curse. Because he is faithful and keeps his promises, God must keep the Mosaic covenant. This means he must punish the sin brought to light by the law.

JESUS CHRIST REDEEMS THE SEED OF ABRAHAM

Jesus is the fulfillment of the promise to Abraham because he took on the curse of the law (3:13–14) in order to redeem the seed of Abraham, all those who by faith are in Christ (3:29). This is a return to the reason of the letter to the Galatians: to go back under the law is to re-enter a covenant which has been finalized, concluded in Christ's death.

The old covenant could only end in death, but since Christ died on behalf of those who were under the curse, those who believe and are in Christ obtain life. This is a new life which is confirmed by the Spirit of God. This is consistent with the Old Testament since it is the Spirit of God who would bring life to dead Israel, restoring them as a nation and making them alive again in the coming kingdom. Ezekiel 37:1–14 is a vivid illustration of the future resurrection of Israel as a nation. In that prophecy Ezekiel sees Israel as dead, dry bones. It is not until the Lord brings them back to life and breathes his Spirit into them that they are alive again. It is this life-giving activity of the Holy Spirit which will characterize the coming age. But in Ezekiel 37 there is no future hope for the Gentiles.

A Future Israel with Gentiles

While the idea of a future restoration of the people of God is found throughout the Old Testament, there are several things here which are unique to Paul. First, Gentiles will be included in this restoration apart from law. They do not "convert to Israel," nor are they totally annihilated as enemies of God.

Second, Israel is not excluded in favor of the Gentiles. There is no replacement theology here. Paul is still Jewish and still believes there is much advantage to being a Jew (Rom 9:1-6). But the "body of Christ" is neither Jew nor Gentile (Gal 3:28). The old "us versus them" categories do not apply in this new age of grace.

Third, while the life-giving Spirit does usher in a new "age of the Spirit," it is not the messianic kingdom expected by other Jewish writers in the Second Temple period. Paul does not deny a future for Israel (Rom 9-11), but this future kingdom is not Paul's topic in the book of Galatians.

Fourth, because of the purpose of the law, it no longer has an application in the present age of the Spirit. This is the problem in the Galatian churches. Gentile Christians are trying to live in an age which no longer exists. It is not just that there is no benefit to keeping the law, but it is actually counterproductive to life in the Spirit to try to live under the law.

Last, and looking ahead to the last two chapters of Galatians, life in the Spirit, or a life of freedom in Christ, means one is free from the constraints of the law. But there are still ethical and moral duties as a member of the family of God. One is not "free from the law" so that sin may abound; one is "free from the law" in order to serve others (5:13).

Conclusion

Most people enjoy a tangible list of achievements they can point to as demonstrating their success. Think back to my analogy from college. Imagine what would happen if a student with a few business classes from a city college tried to claim their academic achievements were good enough to graduate with an MBA from Harvard Business School. Harvard would reject their application to graduate because they did not conform to the standards of the university.

To a certain extent, this is what the agitators are trying to do in Galatia. They are encouraging the Gentiles to follow the wrong requirements. They are the wrong requirements because God is not saving people under the old covenant anymore. It is therefore dangerous to return to the old covenant as a basis for salvation after the finished work of Jesus Christ on the cross.

QUESTIONS FOR FURTHER DISCUSSION

1. What does the law teach us about God's character?
2. What are some examples of "tangible lists of achievement" Christians try to use today in order to demonstrate their spiritual development?
3. In what ways can legalism in the church create divisions between insiders and outsiders? How can these boundary markers hinder the gospel?

9

Being Children of God
Galatians 3:23—4:7

INTRODUCTION

THERE HAVE BEEN A number of popular movies featuring a nanny who comes to a troubled family and helps them through a difficult time. In Mary Poppins, for example, this wonderful guardian is hired by the family and helps everyone become a better person before floating away on the wind. But that is not how the character appears in the Mary Poppins books. P. L. Travers described Mary Poppins as an intimidating and stern person who insisted the children obey. In fact, most literary nannies are indeed quite scary!

In this section Paul describes a transition in salvation history, from law to grace, by using the metaphor of a stern guardian. This would have been a vivid image for the original readers, but modern readers may misunderstand Paul's point since we do not have a similar role in our culture. Using the modern "babysitter" or "nanny" is not really enough to appreciate the depth of Paul's metaphor, and "tutor" or "guide" might say more than Paul intends. If we unpack this metaphor in the way in which Paul intended, then the law was temporary and the present age is the time of maturity in the Spirit.

BEING CHILDREN OF GOD

AN ANALOGY: THE LAW AS GUARDIAN (3:23–4:7)

Paul describes the law as a guardian or supervisor (3:23–26; 4:1–3).[1] This is a metaphor drawn from the well-known practice in the Greco-Roman world of assigning a slave to assist in raising one's children from the age of six to the late teen years. Typically a wealthy family would purchase a slave and assign him to the role of pedagogue.

What Is a Pedagogue?

Often the pedagogue was a captured soldier with some education, but was too old to work. The guardian was not a teacher, although they may have assisted with learning. They were responsible for taking the child to his teacher and would keep him focused during his studies, often sometimes with a stick! In addition, the pedagogue was to be the moral guide for the child. Since a child was thought to be ruled by passions rather than by reason, the pedagogue was to help the child to keep his passions under control and to teach the child how to live by reason. Plato described the pedagogue as a horse's bridle which restricted the natural passions of the child (*Laws* 808e). Once a child "came of age," there was no longer a need for a pedagogue and the child was "free" from their guardian. While a pedagogue may still be respected and honored, after the young man has reached maturity, the relationship ought to end.

In the literature of the Greco-Roman world, a pedagogue was sometimes characterized as rude, cantankerous, and generally rough on their charges. With respect to sexual morals, the pedagogue was a "strict kill-joy." "Whipping or a cuff often accompanied a pedagogue's commands."[2] Literature, however, does not always reflect reality. It is unlikely all Victorian-era British nannies

---

1. Much of this material is drawn from Norman Young, "PAIDAGOGOS: The Social Setting of a Pauline Metaphor."
2. Young, "PAIDAGOGOS," 162.

were as wretched as they appear in literature or film. Sometimes they are witches; other times they are practically perfect in every way.

Understanding a Metaphor

However, Paul is not emphasizing every aspect of a life under a pedagogue. Metaphors usually highlight some things while other things remain in the background. For example, simply because some Greek literature describes the guardian as a slave driver does not mean Paul wants to describe the law as a slave driver. The main point of the metaphor is the role of the guardian is temporary. When the child reaches maturity, the guardian no longer necessary and it is foolish to continue to live under the pedagogue's guardianship any longer.

Paul claims the Galatian believers are too old to rely upon their pedagogue any longer. They have reached the age of maturity and they no longer need the control the pedagogue provided. If this is true, then it is simply inappropriate to try to live under the rule of the pedagogue. Imagine a college graduate who wants to return to his second-grade classroom and live under the "rule" of a second-grade teacher once again. Most people would think this is strange at the very least (and it will probably result in a restraining order). Likewise, for Paul it is simply unimaginable a person would want to live under the guardianship of the law; the believer is now mature because of the work of Christ on the cross.

REACHING MATURITY

In Galatians 4:1 Paul extends his analogy of a child growing to maturity to a child who has "come of age." If a child is an heir, he cannot access his legacy until he reaches maturity. Until then he is under the authority of a guardian and has the same rights as a slave. It is the father who sets up these authorities to guide the child until he is mature. Paul wants to show that God designed the law to act as a guide for God's people until they come into their maturity. When maturity arrives, they will no longer be under law. Instead, they will be guided by the Holy Spirit. In fact, Paul describes this leading of the Spirit later in Galatians with a word related to a pedagogue.

An End for the Law

Galatians 3:25 is particularly radical for a Jew living in the first century. Paul says "we are no longer under the guardian," that is, law. Since Paul includes himself in this verse, is he claiming the Jews are no longer law? This seems to be the correct reading of the text, although this would be an extremely radical statement for a first-century Jew to make.

This is what puts Paul at odds not only with his opponents in the Galatian churches but also with someone like James. Until Paul, no Jew would have suggested the law is no longer applicable. But here Paul goes further, saying the law's time of guardianship is over and the mature person is the one who is "in Christ." The one who is "in Christ" is no longer under law. Perhaps this is the reason why James is so careful with Paul when he returns to Jerusalem in Acts 21:17–26. If people read only the letter of Galatians or heard of Paul's teaching (or worse, heard rumors of what Paul might be teaching), it would be easy to accuse him of breaking the law.

TO BE CLOTHED IN CHRIST

Paul knows the time of the law is over (3:27–29). If a person has been "baptized in Christ," then they have "put on Christ." To be "baptized into Christ" is a regular metaphor in Paul's letters for new birth in Christ. Titus 3:5–6, for example, describes regeneration as the washing of the Spirit. When we pass from death to life we are reborn and regenerated by the Holy Spirit.

In the context of Galatians, it is impossible Paul could be talking about the ritual of water baptism. Paul has argued throughout the book the ritual of circumcision has no spiritual value in the present age. It would undercut his argument entirely if he now claimed baptism had some sort of spiritual value. If circumcision has no value for salvation, then neither does baptism. Paul is certainly not replacing circumcision with baptism here!

By receiving the Holy Spirit, Paul says, the believer has "put on Christ." To put on Christ is a synonym for conversion (3:27). The verb is in the aorist tense, indicating an event which has already taken place. Being clothed in Christ is a regular metaphor in the Pauline letters for righteous living. In Colossians 3:12 the believer is to be "clothed" with a set of virtues and in Ephesians 6:11–17 the believer is to put on the "whole armor of God."

Social Distinctions No Longer Matter

"In Christ" there is no Jew or Greek, slave or free, male or female (3:28). The believer's new status in Christ makes all previous social distinctions meaningless. This includes ethnic and social distinctions. The first of the three pairs of relationships is ethnic (Jew nor Greek) and they are most appropriate for Paul's argument. If one is "in Christ," it does not matter if one is born a Jew or a Gentile. There is therefore no reason to convert to Judaism, since there is no difference in Christ.

This is potentially the most radical thing Paul has said so far in this letter. For the agitators, the Gentiles are becoming part of Israel. They are Jews, no longer Gentiles. Paul's claim is the opposite: when one has "put on Christ," ethnic distinctions no longer matter. There is no longer an advantage to being Jewish or a disadvantage to being Gentile.

The second pair (slave nor free) breaks down one of the most important social distinctions in the ancient word: the relationship between a free person and a slave. In any of Paul's churches both slaves and free people would worship together. A slave owner was no more important in the body of Christ than a slave. It is difficult for the modern reader to grasp the difference this would have made in the Christian churches.

The third pair is perhaps the more surprising since virtually every culture makes a distinction between male and female. It is possible Paul's opponents argued a woman ought to be married to a man who was properly keeping the law in order to be "fully Christian." Women could be considered less spiritually advanced since they could not fully keep the law in the same way men could. Women worshiped separately from the men in the synagogue, yet in the body of Christ men and women are both equally free in Christ and ought to worship together.

All three of these pairs are "natural" circumstances of birth. In Jewish or Greco-Roman society, what matters for your standing in society is your birth. For Paul, what matters is your new birth, who you are in Christ. The reason these social distinctions no longer matter is that the one who is "in Christ" by faith is now the offspring of Abraham. We are now the same family, therefore ethnic and social distinctions no longer matter.

A New Family

The idea of family is important in both Jewish and Greco-Roman cultures. The bonds between brothers were more important than the bonds of marriage. Family always came first in ancient cultures. Like Jesus before him (Mark 3:31–34), Paul says God is creating a new family which transcends human family. The members of the churches at Galatia are part of a family now, the family of Abraham, and that new relationship in Christ is more important than earthly family distinctions. The body of Christ as a family is the foundation for the argument Paul is making in Galatians. If we are "in Christ," then we are a new creation. But more than that, we are part of a new family, adopted by God and therefore responsible to our new family. The old family should be left behind because only the new family matters now.

Paul describes a shift in salvation history from the law to Christ (4:4–7). "At just the right time" Christ came into the world. This might be taken as the ideal time for Jesus to be born, politically speaking. But Paul says Christ came at the "time which God planned." The purpose of Jesus life was to redeem those under the law (a form of slavery, 4:1–3) and to provide for their adoption as dearly loved children of God. Since we are children of God we are also heirs of God, a theme Paul will pick up later in chapter 4.

CONCLUSION

It would be strange for an adult to want to live like a child again. No mature person should need to have a nanny hovering over them telling them what they should do. For Paul, the time of the law has come to an end in Christ. It is therefore inappropriate for a person to go back to the law in order to be right with God. Since Jesus has provided full justification before God through faith in his death and resurrection, attempting to keep the law again is foolish. Christians are living in the new age of the Spirit; they are adopted into God's family as dearly loved children and not slaves to the law. Therefore, we ought to act like who we are: the children of God.

QUESTIONS FOR FURTHER DISCUSSION

1. What are some ways the law functioned as a guardian for Israel in the Old Testament?
2. How does the modern church make social distinctions similar to the ethnic and social boundaries in Galatians 3:28? What are some ways the church can work to break down these boundaries?
3. What are the social and ethical implications of being a part of a "new family" in Christ?

10

Stop Acting Like a Slave
Galatians 4:8–20

INTRODUCTION

THESE VERSES SHOW PAUL'S pastoral concern for the Galatian churches. They are returning to a time in salvation history when they were slaves and not enjoying their rights as children of God. Paul reminds the churches of the joy with which they received the gospel in the first place—what has happened to that joy (4:15)?

SLAVES BY NATURE (4:8-11)

In Galatians 4:1–7 Paul makes a contrast between a child who is an heir and a slave. When someone is justified by God's grace through faith, they are adopted into God's family and are therefore children of God. All the social distinctions of the old life no longer have any value; the only thing that matters is being "in Christ." What concerns Paul is the Galatians' desire to turn their backs on their new status as children of God and become slaves once again.

Enslaved by Nature

Paul is clearly addressing Gentile readers who at one time did not know the one true God of Israel. The Greco-Roman world certainly did not know the God of Israel. But amazingly there are a number of passages in the Old Testament describing Israel as having no knowledge of God. In Hosea 4:1, for example, there as "no knowledge of God in the land" just prior to the exile of Israel.

The Gentiles were "by nature" enslaved to pagan gods. In Galatians 2:15 Paul uses the same word for himself and Peter, who are "Jews by birth," and in Ephesians 2:3 he describes all people as "by nature" children of wrath. The word refers to a person's natural disposition or inclination. This inclination is so strong it might be described as an "addiction." People who are addicted to certain behaviors have an overwhelming desire to practice their addiction. This may be a simple addiction to social media (try to pry someone's cell phone out of their hand). For Paul, humans are born with an addiction to worship anything and everything except the creator God. The whole Gentile world is designed to reinforce slavery to the gods.

Elementary Principles

These gods are only "elementary principles."[1] Paul uses this phrase here and in Colossians 2:8 and 2:20, although it is not clear what he means by it. In the Greco-Roman world, these principles are the fundamental elements which are really in charge of this world. This could refer to the planets and stars, since astrology and celestial signs were important throughout the ancient world. The elementary principles could also refer to spiritual beings thought to control the lives of ordinary people. Every home would have household gods (*lares*) who supposedly protected the family and ensured wealth and success. The father of the clan would be responsible for honoring the family gods to ensure the success of

---

1. Bundrick, "*Ta Stoicheia Tou Kosmou.*"

his family. For many Jews, these gods and spirits were considered demonic forces.

A third possibility is that the "elementary principles" may simply be the natural tendency of all cultures to worship gods of some kind. This last suggestion is likely since Paul applies elementary principles to both the gods worshiped by the Gentiles before coming to faith in Christ as well as the practices from the law now tempting the Gentiles. It is hard to imagine, however, Paul referring to the practice of Sabbath as a demonic force.

To the Gentile world, these elementary principles may appear to have power, but they are in fact weak. Paul describes the gods of the Gentiles as poor, shabby gods. This description of the pagan gods is similar to Paul's brief sermon in Acts 14:15. After Paul was thought to be the god Hermes, he calls the gods "worthless." Even if the elemental principles are demonic, they are nothing at all compared to the creator God who has called the Galatian believers to a new life in Christ. By attempting to keep the law, the Gentiles would re-enslave themselves the elementary powers. As Dunn says, even if they are turning to the elementary principles of the law, the Gentiles are ironically turning from the God of the law.[2]

Days, Months, Seasons, and Years

Since all ancient religions had feasts and sacred days, one of the most attractive parts of the law for the Gentile was the variety of special days. When they worshiped worthless gods, the Galatian Gentiles followed a sacred calendar which included a variety of feast days and celebrations. When they turned from those gods to the living and true God, they also gave up the sacred calendar. At this point in history, Christianity did not have anything like the feasts and celebrations which were popular in the Greco-Roman or Jewish world.

By "days" Paul refers to the Sabbath. Keeping the Sabbath was critically important in first-century Jewish practice. The day of rest

2. Dunn, *Galatians*, 225.

was considered by non-Jews to be a most peculiar practice and one which could be exploited. The Romans took advantage of the Jews' refusal to fight on the Sabbath to build earthworks near Jerusalem's walls (*War* 1.15–147). In Diaspora Jewish communities it was common for a Jew to be taken to court on the Sabbath, hoping they would not appear to defend themselves (*Antiq.* 16.45–46). Greek and Roman writers regularly mocked the Jews for the practice of the Sabbath.

"Months" refers to new moon celebrations. Numbers 28:11–15 describes the sacrifices for the new moon celebration (known as Rosh Chodesh). When the new moon was first observed, shofars signaled the beginning of the celebration. Business was to cease even if the day was not the Sabbath (Amos 8:5) and a number of sacrifices were made at the temple. For Jews living in the Diaspora, the day was marked with prayers in the synagogue along with reciting Psalms 113–18.

By "seasons" Paul probably has in mind the three major feasts in the law. Passover, Pentecost, and Tabernacles (Pesach, Shavuot, and Sukkot) were occasions for Jews to travel to Jerusalem and participate in worship at the temple. It would not be possible for Jews living outside of Judea to regularly participate in these pilgrimages, so worship at the synagogue took the place of travelling to Jerusalem. Passover developed into a family celebration to remember God's redemption of Israel out of Egypt.

Paul's reference to "years" is more problematic, since it is unlikely Jews living outside of Judea would attempt to practice the Sabbath year. It is more likely this refers to the often contentious calendar issues within Judaism. There were some factions such as the Qumran community who followed a solar calendar (365 days), but the temple used a lunar calendar (360 days). This is not a minor difference between the groups since following the wrong calendar meant Sabbaths and feast days would fall at the wrong times. One could be breaking the Day of Atonement fast without knowing it.

Part of the attraction of the Jewish sacred calendar for Gentile converts was the familiarity of a religious calendar. It gave them something to mark out their lives and feel like they were practicing a religion at least similar to the rest of the Greco-Roman world. While it was easy to follow the Sabbath traditions, Paul sees all this as a return to slavery. In fact, Paul is afraid he had labored in vain when he established the Galatian churches. "In vain" is an adverb which refers to an action which has no success or profit. Not only are these practices a return to slavery, they have no value with respect to obtaining salvation.

BE LIKE PAUL (4:12-16)

After wondering if his work in Galatia was in vain, Paul makes a very personal appeal to the Galatian believers. He wants them to be like he was during his first visit. In what sense does Paul want them to "become like him"? Paul is a Jew who understands the place of the law in the present age and he is no longer relying on the law for his salvation (1 Cor 9:21). The Gentile believers, on the other hand, were never under the law yet now they want to rely on it for their salvation.

Remember My Weakness

Paul recalls his experience when he first preached the gospel in Galatia. When Paul first preached the gospel to them he was weak in his flesh, but they did not despise him on account of his condition. To what is Paul referring in verses 13-14? First, it is important to observe Paul often describes himself as weak in order to highlight his reliance on God. In 2 Corinthians 12:10 Paul states he is content in all of his weakness and afflictions because he knows when he is weak, God is strong.

Second, Paul says this particular weakness was a trial to the Galatians. It is possible Paul meant his weakness "put you to the test" or even that his weakness was a kind of temptation for the believers in Galatia. If Paul had a serious physical problem it could be interpreted as a curse or even the work of an evil spirit. Some scholars have suggested the agitators used Paul's physical weakness as a proof he was under the curse of the law. Illness and disease was often associated with sin in the Old Testament. Deuteronomy 28:22 specifically links physical illness with breach of the law.

Third, the Galatian believers did not reject Paul or treat him with disrespect as a result of this weakness. The verb has the connotation of treating something with contempt, especially when coupled with spitting. But Dunn points out the word Paul chose for spitting refers to warding off evil spirits.[3] Earlier in the letter Paul wondered if the Galatians had been "bewitched" (3:1).

Paul describes his "thorn in the flesh" in similar terms in 2 Corinthians 12:7. Paul says he is being harassed by some sort of messenger from Satan. The noun Paul uses in 2 Corinthians refers to a violent physical beating and is the same word used for beating Jesus in Matthew 26:67. Since it is not clear what Paul means by this thorn, scholars have suggested the beatings are not physical but perhaps severe headaches, eye trouble, or malaria. Since Galatians 4:15 says the church would have "gouged out their eyes" for Paul, many have associated Paul's illness as some sort of eye problem.

You Received Me as an Angel

Despite having the appearance of a man cursed by the gods or under a demonic influence, the Galatians received Paul and his gospel positively. It is not a coincidence that Paul describes his reception as "like an angel." The Greek word for angel can be translated as "messenger." In Acts 14:11–13 the people of Lystra thought Paul was Hermes, the "messenger of the gods." This subtle allusion to the events of Acts 14 and may explain the source of Paul's weakness. After he convinced the crowd he was not a god, Paul was taken outside the city of Lystra, stoned, and left for dead (Acts 14:19–30).

If the Galatian churches remember this event, then they know Paul was attacked by people from the synagogue who opposed

---

3. Dunn, *Galatians*, 234.

Stop Acting Like a Slave

Paul's message to the Gentiles. Paul has "become like them" since he faced the same contempt from the Jews and he suffered persecution because of his preaching of the gospel of God's Grace to the Gentiles. Yet despite their close bond, Paul now feels as though the Galatians have become his enemies.

Now I Am Like an Enemy

Is it the influence of the agitators which has changed the minds of the Galatians and made Paul into an enemy? The combination of "enemy" and "zealous" in verses 16–17 is not a coincidence. When commenting on his own persecution of the church, Paul describes himself as "zealous" for the traditions of his fathers (1:14). Like Phineas or Elijah in the Old Testament, this zeal took the form of a violent response to the Jewish Christians in Jerusalem. Paul claims the agitators are zealous on behalf of the churches in Galatia and have turned Paul into the enemy.

Like Paul prior to his Damascus road experience, the agitators are also zealous for the traditions of their fathers, especially the boundary markers of Judaism. By insisting on these markers, the agitators can show the Gentile believers they have not done everything they ought to in order to be right with God.

In fact, these boundaries effectively keep the Gentiles from joining the people of God! The agitators want to "shut out" or exclude the Gentiles who have accepted God's grace through the preaching of Paul. The word means "lock out," as if the agitators insist on observance of the law in order to lock the door of salvation to the Gentiles. During the Jewish War the Zealots who controlled the temple excluded anyone who did not agree with them from participation in a festival (*J.W.* 2.425). Paul's real problem in the Antioch incident (2:11–14) is that Gentiles are treated as second-class members of the church. Since they have not crossed over the boundary set by the "men from James" they are not fully justified and are still sinners.

The agitator's zeal for the Galatians is for "no good purpose," but Paul's zeal for the church is positive. Passionate zeal can be positive if it is channeled to good things, but the agitators are passionate for the wrong reasons. By their insistence in the law, they force the Gentiles to fully convert or no longer be a part of the church.

Although this is not altogether obvious from the text, it is possible the Gentiles would have been expelled from their own congregations if they did not submit to circumcision, food traditions, and Sabbath. If this is the case, then Paul's purpose here is to prevent them not from becoming Jews, but from returning to paganism! Paul fears his children in the faith may walk away from their relationship with Jesus Christ.

THE PAINS OF CHILDBIRTH (4:18-20)

Paul cares for the churches in Galatia like a parent for their dearly loved child. The metaphor of a parent appears in 1 Thessalonians 2 and is not unusual in the Greco-Roman world for the relationship of a teacher and his disciples. What is unique here is Paul's description of the pain he feels over the situation in Galatia. His pain is like childbirth!

This pain usually refers to a woman giving birth, but is occasionally used for apocalyptic troubles effecting the world prior to the return of Jesus. For Paul to apply this metaphor to himself indicates the extremity of his emotional pain over the possible defection of Gentiles in the Galatian churches. Paul often describes salvation as new life; here he pictures his ministry in Galatia as a mother enduring difficult labor bringing a child into the world. It is true he was persecuted and did in fact endure great pain in order to bring the gospel to the region.

Paul will endure this pain until "Christ is formed in you." This is an unusual choice of words, but "formed" is an extension of the birth metaphor, although now it is the Galatian believers who are "giving birth." This metaphor could refer to individual believers who have accepted Jesus Christ and are personally growing into the image of Christ. On the other hand, Paul may have in mind the whole community of believers who mature into the image of Christ.

When a mother gives birth there is a great deal of pain, but this is only the beginning of the difficult task of raising a child. There are many years and a great deal more pain before a child grows to maturity. Like a parent raising a child, Paul will not stop enduring pain until the churches in Galatia reach the goal of maturity in Christ. The current situation is painful for Paul since he must speak sternly to his dearly loved children in order to help them understand they are putting themselves at risk by listening to the agitators.

CONCLUSION

Paul's wish is to be present with the churches again, since he is perplexed by their desire to keep the Jewish law. As he says in Galatians 4:20, he wishes he could be present in their congregation so he might "change his tone" and speak with them as a loving parent. Written words can be misunderstood, and Paul has written some very difficult things in this letter. If he visited the churches in Galatia personally it would be far easier to communicate his message.

Paul is perplexed by the Gentiles in Galatia who are considering accepting the agitator's message and submitting to the law. For Paul, this is a confusing course of action and he cannot imagine why they would want to submit themselves again to a form of slavery now that they have experienced the freedom of the grace of God.

QUESTIONS FOR FURTHER DISCUSSION

1. What is the purpose of creating boundaries? Is it to define who is "in" the group or to keep people outside?

2. Are there examples in the modern church where Christians adopt more-or-less secular practices in order to be more comfortable in the church?

3. What does it mean to have "Christ formed" in us? What does this look like for an individual, or for a whole community of believers?

11

Sarah and Hagar
Galatians 4:21—5:1

INTRODUCTION

THIS IS THE FINAL stage in Paul's scriptural argument against the agitators in the Galatian churches. He has made the point that Abraham was justified before he submitted to circumcision rather than after. In fact, Abraham was right with God before the law was given at all. In this section Paul begins an allegorical argument based on the two wives and two children of Abraham.

This is one of the most difficult passages in all of the Pauline letters for several reasons. First, Paul uses a method which is simply not familiar to us. He seems to draw things out of the text we would not find there in the first place. If a modern pastor made this sort of an argument from an Old Testament story, most people would object to his reasoning based on the use of allegory alone. But Paul did not intend this passage to be a model for how to interpret Scripture, although it was a legitimate way to draw implications from Old Testament stories used by Jews in the first century.

Second, the allegory itself seems strange to the modern reader since it is not a modern allegory at all. For example, in *The*

Chronicles of Narnia it is obvious C. S. Lewis intended Aslan to represent Jesus in some ways. John Bunyan's *Pilgrim's Progress* is an example of an obvious allegory. But the story Paul uses from Genesis was not intended as an allegory in the first place. Paul is creating a contrast between the two sons of Abraham, one who was born free, and the other who was born in slavery. While the story in Genesis is not an allegory, Paul is drawing an allegorical application from it.

AN ALLEGORY: ABRAHAM HAD TWO WIVES

Paul begins by telling his readers to listen to the law (4:21). He addresses those in the Galatian churches who want to keep the law. The tense of the verb implies the Galatian believers want to submit to law, but have not yet done so. It is as if Paul is saying, "If you want to keep the law, understand what it is saying to you before you submit to circumcision."

Why does Paul select Genesis 21 for the conclusion of his argument? It is possible the agitators in his churches used this text to encourage the Gentile believers to be circumcised in order to fully convert to Judaism. Isaac was the child of the promise, but Ishmael was expelled from the camp. If Ishmael is the father of all Gentiles in this allegory, then the agitators could have used this text to insist Gentiles must convert to Judaism in order to be right with God.

If this is the case, then "listen to the law" actually refers to the hearing of the law as it was being taught in the Galatian churches. It is highly unlikely any Gentile in the Galatian churches could have read the law in Hebrew, although a Greek translation may have been available. Even then, they would only know the law through hearing it read in church meetings. If the agitators selected texts like Genesis 17 (Abraham is commanded to circumcise his children) and Genesis 21 (children of Ishmael are excluded from the promise), then it is possible Gentiles were told these passages command they submit to circumcision to be fully right with God.

SARAH AND HAGAR

Paul refers to the story of Sarah and Hagar as an allegory, although he is using an allegorical method in order to make the Genesis story apply to the Galatian situation. In other words, Paul's way of reading Genesis here is more like an application or an analogy rather than a full allegorization of the original story.

The readers of Galatians need to recall not just individual verses from Genesis 21 but the whole plot of the Abraham stories in Genesis. God promised to make Abraham into a great nation, despite the fact he was childless. Since his wife Sarah was old and barren, Abraham has a child by his wife's handmaid Hagar. The culture at the time would have accepted this as a legitimate method for having an heir, but it was not God's plan. God eventually gives Sarah a natural child (Gen 21:1–7). Hagar's son, Ishmael, realizes he will not be the heir once Isaac is born to Sarah, and he begins to harass his brother. Eventually Sarah forces Hagar and Ishmael to leave Abraham's tents (Gen 21:8–21). In the story, Isaac is the legitimate heir to the promise. Ishmael is not the heir and was sent away from the blessing of Abraham's family.

TWO COVENANTS

Paul draws a series of contrasts from this story in Galatians 4:22–26. Since this is typical of an allegorical reading in first-century rhetoric, Paul's point would have been something the original readers would have expected and appreciated. The two women represent two covenants, one given to Abraham in Genesis 12 and another covenant given to Moses at Mount Sinai. Hagar is called a slave in the Greek translation of Genesis 21, but Sarah is never called a "free woman." This implies Paul is highlighting only one aspect of the story and drawing an inference from the contrast between the women. This contrast is one of Paul's more radical contributions to Christian theology since there is nothing similar to this two-covenant view in first-century Judaism.

Paul conceives of the two covenants as separate covenants, while the agitators see the Mosaic covenant as an extension of the Abrahamic. If this is what the agitators are saying, there are some serious implications. If the Mosaic covenant is the same as the Abrahamic covenant, then those who are "in Christ" are also under law and ought to submit to the boundary markers of circumcision, food, and Sabbath laws. But if the law was given between the promise and the present age of the Spirit, then the law is not "for this age."

Three Ages of God's Plan

Paul has three ages in mind in Galatians: from Abraham to the law (promise), from the law to the fulfillment of the law "in Christ" (law), and the present age of the Holy Spirit (grace). Sarah represents the first covenant or age, Hagar the second age, and the third age could be described as the "new covenant" (2 Cor 3). In other letters Paul adds a fourth age, an age "yet to come" (Eph 1:21, the kingdom of God). The problem in Galatians does not require him to discuss any future ages, so he simply does not mention it here.

Paul also contrasts the Abrahamic and Mosaic covenants by drawing a parallel between the earthly Jerusalem and heavenly Jerusalem. Paul connects the old covenant of the law with Mount Sinai (v. 25). Mount Sinai is outside of the land and in Hagar's territory from the perspective of Genesis 21. The new covenant, on the other hand, was enacted in the "real" Jerusalem, in heaven (v. 26).

The fact Paul considers Jerusalem to be under the yoke of slavery is significant. He could be referring to the fact Jerusalem is still under Roman rule (and the exile continues), but it is more likely Paul is dismissing the earthly Jerusalem because the agitators make a great deal about their connection to the Jerusalem church.

What is surprising is that Hagar represents those who are enslaved by the law, or Second Temple–period Judaism! Sarah is a free woman in the Genesis story, so she represents those who are saved apart from the law. Going back to verse 19, Paul describes his ministry as "bearing free children" like Sarah, while the agitators are "bearing slave children" like Hagar. It is all they are capable of since they are still under the yoke of the law. This is an ironic twist in Paul's application of the two women, since no Jewish person in the first century would appreciate being called a "child of Ishmael."

BE GLAD, BARREN WOMAN!

Finally, Paul quotes Isaiah 54:1 to complete his argument (v. 27). But why does he choose this text and apply it to Sarah and Hagar? How does this verse apply to the Galatian situation?

The original context of the verses is the return from the exile. At some point in the future, Isaiah says, Israel will return from the exile and gather again in Zion (Jerusalem). Isaiah uses the metaphor of a woman who has lost her husband and her children. The woman represents Jerusalem after it has been destroyed and the inhabitants scattered throughout the world in the exile. When the exile is over, Lady Zion will be restored to her marriage and her children will return to her. She will once again rejoice in her restored marriage and family. Paul has in mind the whole of Isaiah 40–55, but especially 51:1–3, the only place in the Old Testament that refers to Sarah as a mother. Paul is drawing Genesis 21 together with Isaiah 51:1–3 based on this fact in order to show that what is happening in the present age is an eschatological fulfillment of Isaiah.

Paul applies this verse to the Gentiles who are coming to faith in Jesus the Messiah. Lady Zion will have more children than before, and they will be freeborn children, born apart from the law. This may imply the Pauline churches have more converts than the Jerusalem churches at this point in history, or they will very soon. Pauline Christianity does finally overwhelm the agitators and even the Jewish Christians in Jerusalem.

If this is true, however, then there might be a hint that within twenty years of the crucifixion so many Gentiles have come to faith in Christ that Paul can describe his churches as a "more than the original family." Paul's conclusion, then, is the one who is "in Christ" is a child of Sarah, like Isaac, and not a child of the slave Hagar. He has reversed the teaching of the agitators to demonstrate that those who are free are not under the slavery of the law.

WE ARE CHILDREN OF THE FREE WOMAN (4:28-31)

Finally, Paul draws an inference from the allegory. If those who are in Christ are the true heir, the false heir, Ishmael, must be put out of the camp (4:29-30). Paul still has the original story in mind. Abraham was forced to expel Hagar and Ishmael to protect Isaac, the child of the promise. The one born "according to the flesh" (Ishmael) persecuted the "one born of the Spirit." "Born of the Spirit" is a reference to the miraculous birth of Isaac and provides the hook for Paul's contrast. The ones who are "in Christ" are born of the Spirit, returning to the point where he began this argument in Galatians 3:1-6.

Persecution?

Just as Ishmael persecuted Isaac, the Galatian believers are in danger from the agitators, the "children of slavery." Does Paul have a literal persecution in mind here? This is possible since Galatians 3:4 implies the Gentile believers have already "suffered many things." But the real danger may be inderailing their faith by submitting to the law. Reading ahead in the letter, there is a serious danger to one's faith if he submits to law (5:1-2, for example). This may be the reason for the warning to expel the threat in the church.

Paul is playing the role of Sarah and commanding the agitators be expelled from the church. In verse 19 Paul describes the church as his little children. He declares his concern for the church is like the "anguish of childbirth." As strange as it sounds, Paul is speaking the words of Sarah to the Galatian churches.

The Danger of Allowing Ishmael to Remain

The agitators must be removed because there is danger in allowing them to remain. Like Ishmael, they threaten the (spiritual) life of the true heirs of Abraham. This seems strong by contemporary standards, but for Paul this is critical to the health of the church.

The agitators are attacking what it means to be "in Christ" and therefore risk destroying the church. As he will say in 5:9–10, the bad yeast must be wholly removed and thrown away if the church is to remain healthy.

Remarkably, Paul includes himself as an heir of the free woman (v. 31) since it is only believers in Jesus who are children of the free woman. This may be a hint Paul considered himself free from the law, despite what he says in Acts 23:1. In the first two chapters of this letter Paul described himself as separate from the Jerusalem church. It is impossible to know if Paul's "all things to all men" ministry model allowed him to break traditional boundary makers such as travel on the Sabbath or food taboos. While Paul cannot be considered anti-law, he is certainly pro-freedom in Christ.

THEREFORE, STAND FIRM (5:1)

This verse serves as a conclusion to the argument of chapters 3 and 4, but also as an introduction to the final section of the book. Beginning in 3:1 Paul has argued the one who is "in Christ" is free from the law, which he now describes as a "yoke of slavery." When Paul says it is for freedom that Christ set us free, he is referring to a practice of purchasing a slave in order to set that slave free. This resonates with what Paul says in Romans 6:15–18: the one who is "in Christ" is no longer a slave, but a free child of God. It simply does not make sense, Paul says, to serve the old master as a slave again, whether the "old master" is the law or sin!

If a slave has been set free, it makes sense he would continue to live free rather than submit again to the old master. Paul therefore tells his readers to "stand firm" in the freedom they have in Jesus Christ. It is far too easy to submit to a form of legalism and then look to one's own spiritual accomplishments to demonstrate one's commitment to God.

CONCLUSION

It takes a serious effort not to live like a slave. Paul does not want to encourage sin, but be must emphasize the believer's status before God as a dearly loved child. The one who is "in Christ" should respond to God as a child responds to their parent. A child wants to please their parents, although they often fail to do so. The loving parent knows this and is happy the child is trying to do what is right.

No one should ever feel guilty because they have failed to be a perfect Christian. If you are "in Christ," you are already a perfect Christian. You cannot do anything to be more justified or more "right with God." If you are "in Christ," all you have to do is be "in Christ." For Gentiles to attempt to submit to the law would be to return to a yoke of slavery. Paul is therefore urging his readers to simply "be what they are," true heirs of the promise, not children under the care of the guardian.

This obviously raises some problems for Paul. Someone might have thought, "If I do not have to act morally, why should I?" For the Jewish convert, this probably was not an issue since the Jewish law has extremely high moral content. But there are some behaviors which may be acceptable to the Gentile which are offensive to God. There are some moral behaviors not appropriate for "children of God." If Paul tells his congregations to not keep the law, how will Paul encourage the Gentile converts to behave in a way which pleases the Father? This is the burden of the last two chapters of the book of Galatians.

QUESTIONS FOR FURTHER DISCUSSION

1. In what ways do legalists "persecute" today?
2. Are there examples of legalism damaging the health of a church? In what ways can a church guard against this sort of damage?

3. How does Paul's metaphor of a child help us understand our salvation?

4. How do we "stand firm" in our freedom in Christ?

12

Freedom in Christ
Galatians 5:1–12

INTRODUCTION

THE COLLEGE YEARS ARE often very difficult because for the first time a young adult is free from the restraints associated with living with their parents. Most people have heard of the "freshman fifteen," the amount of weight a freshman in college gains because they are free to eat whatever they want any time they want. Since Mom is not there to tell them they cannot have a third dessert or eat an entire box of Lucky Charms for dinner, many freshman put on a bit of weight.

Paul must deal with a similar problem for his "law-free" gospel in Galatians 5–6. If a person is free from the law, what does God require? Is there another law or set of instructions which the Gentile believer in Christ must follow? Or is the Christian completely free from all restraints?

This is a difficult passage in some ways because Paul is very personal and emotional. Paul drives his point home using rough and jarring language. In fact, he says if the Galatians return to the old covenant, Christ will be of no advantage to them. They are putting themselves in real spiritual danger. Paul's use of shocking language in these verses is calculated and intentional. He is demanding his readers make a decision to stand firm in the gospel now, before they accept circumcision and the law. It will take a conscious decision on the part of the Galatian believers to be "in Christ" and to live in the freedom of their adoption as children of God rather than to return to the now outdated and obsolete covenant of the law.

WHY KEEP THE LAW?

What would be the motivation for Gentiles to adopt Jewish law? Ben Witherington suggests the Galatian believers found themselves in a difficult position. By accepting Jesus as Messiah and Savior, they have turned their backs on the traditional gods of the Greco-Roman world as well as ritual observances associated with those gods.[1] To accept Jesus as Savior is to reject pagan gods.

By rejecting pagan gods, the Gentile converts severed social ties in order to join a religious movement unlike anything else in the ancient world. There are virtually no rituals in the Christian church other than a shared meal which may have included what later became known as Communion (1 Cor 11:17–26). There were no sacrifices or liturgy to follow, nor were there any festivals or feast days. Christianity did not have a temple nor a central gathering place. Keeping the Jewish law at least provided an opportunity for Gentile believers to concretely express their Christian identity. Since Judaism was an ancient religion, Gentile converts embracing Judaism could avoid the charge that they were accepting a strange, new religion.

The Meaning of Rituals

This is one of the most important applications of the book of Galatians to a modern church setting. Very few people would argue Christians ought to be keeping the whole law. But frequently

---

1. Witherington, *Grace in Galatia*, 362.

people assume Christians must do a series of rituals in order to be right with God, such as baptism or Communion. Sometimes the boundary makers are doctrinal. A person must sign a particular doctrinal statement or confession faith. Most people think there are a set of behaviors or lifestyle choices the Christian must adopt in order to act like a Christian.

But Paul never says one must "act like a Christian" in order to be right with God. Someone is right with God by God's grace through faith. They have been adopted into God's family and they are now God's children. In Galatians, Paul is not talking about a new kind of religion but a new kind of relationship with God.

KEEPING LAW ENDANGERS SPIRITUAL LIFE (5:2-6)

The one who tries to keep one part of the law is obligated to keep the whole law (5:2-4). If the members of the Galatian churches accept circumcision, then Christ will be of no advantage. Paul's grammar here suggests the decision is a real possibility at the present time, but one the Galatians have not yet made. They are considering using the law or the Jewish boundary markers as a way of expressing Christian practice.

There is also a future aspect to the second half of the condition. If the Gentile believers fully convert to Judaism, then Christ will be of no continuing benefit to them. This probably does not refer to a future, eschatological judgment. From the moment they accept circumcision, the Gentile believers will put themselves in a place where Christ cannot help them. The reason for this is circumcision represents a return to the old covenant of the law.

Going Backwards

By accepting circumcision as a sign of their new status as Christ-followers, the Gentiles are placing themselves under a covenant which has already expired. The problem is not circumcision, but what circumcision represented: conversion to Judaism and acceptance of the old covenant. Under that covenant, Gentiles need to convert to Judaism to be right with God. Under the new covenant, the Gentiles became a part of something new, a joint body of both Jew and Gentile. The Holy Spirit regenerates the believer and they become a real child of God and an heir of Abraham's promise.

For the Jew or the Gentile, ritual circumcision does not matter. However, Paul did require Timothy to be circumcised in Acts 16:1-4. Even after the Jerusalem council, Paul's ministry among Jews would have been hindered if the Jewish Timothy was left uncircumcised. Titus, on the other hand, was not compelled to be circumcised because he was a Gentile. These two men demonstrate the problem and Paul's solution. Timothy was born under the old covenant, so it was proper for him to submit to circumcision. Titus was never a part of the old covenant so it was inappropriate for him to submit to the ritual.

The reason Paul sees this as a critically important point is because the two covenants are mutually exclusive. As in Galatians 1:6-10, the gospel of the agitators preach is not even a gospel. This is why Paul can say Christ is of no benefit to the Gentiles if they accept the old covenant. The work of Jesus on the cross fulfills that covenant and renders it satisfied; all of its demands have been met.

Only Part of the Law?

Is it possible the agitators did not teach the Gentile converts they had to keep the whole law, but only the boundary markers? It is impossible to know for certain the strategy the agitators used. However, it is likely they did not begin with a command to keep the whole law, but rather only parts of the law. A strategy of gradualism would have been more likely to succeed.

On the one hand, they could have started with the easier traditions, those which were attractive to a Gentile (monotheism, prayer, and Torah study; even the food traditions may have been attractive). Once they have accepted some of the more acceptable traditions and commands, then the agitators could more easily push the Gentiles to circumcision.

Still, Galatians may indeed imply the actual strategy of the agitators was to start with the boundary markers of circumcision, Sabbath, and food laws, then point out that the rest of the law is easy enough to keep after these boundary markers were observed.

Religious Practice

The appeal of the agitators is a practical framework for a new faith in Jesus. There are rituals and practices which mark off one's new life in Christ. If the Galatian believers abstain from certain foods and worship at set times such as the Sabbath, they can have a sense of a "religion." But for Paul, they are not accepting a religion in the Greco-Roman sense, but rather a radically different mode of existence as children of God. This new life in Christ ought to change every aspect of the Gentile's life.

One problem which needs to be addressed here is the point about keeping the whole law. Is it actually true that if one accepts one part of the law they have to keep the whole law? Some scholars consider this Paul's great misunderstanding of the law, or at the very least Paul is overstating his case in order to make his point. There is no real evidence the majority of Judaism in the first century thought it was possible to keep the whole law. Perfect obedience is, however, the requirement of the law itself (Deut 28:58–59). The context is important since this verse stands at the end of the curses and blessings in Deuteronomy. Israel is, at the time Paul wrote Galatians, still in exile as a result of the inability to keep the law. Sirach, a Jewish wisdom book written about 200 B.C., says, "Do not commit a sin twice; not even for one will you go unpunished."

Law and Grace

God has always saved by his grace through the faith of his people. Israel was called to be the people of God and those who really wanted to do God's will obeyed the law to the best of their ability. When they failed, they made appropriate sacrifices with an expectation God's grace would cover their sins. But the fact Israel is still in exile is evidence for Paul that the law was only temporary until God sent his Son to deal with the problem of sin. Paul ironically claims anyone who tries to keep the whole law is committing apostasy, the very sin which put Israel into the exile in the first place. Paul insists trusting in the law for one's justification is a kind of idolatry because it is trusting in something other than Jesus for salvation.

The person who is in Christ can look forward to their final vindication (5:5-6). The verb translated "eagerly await" is always used by Paul to describe the future consummation of our salvation (Phil 3:20; Rom 8:19). Our "hope of righteousness" is a troublesome phrase since the noun translated as "righteousness" is also regularly translated as "justification" or even "vindication." We have been made righteous in Christ and we have been adopted into God's family, but we are not yet resurrected. The problem of sin was solved in Christ's death and resurrection, but we still live in a sinful body in a sinful world. We will be fully glorified at the resurrection (1 Cor 15:51-58), but that resurrection is only possible because of the hope we have through the Spirit, by faith.

By implication, the agitators do not have this hope. By relying on the law for their justification, they have been cut off from the certainty which those who are "in Christ" have by God's grace through faith.

PAUL'S FRUSTRATION WITH THE AGITATORS (5:7-12)

Paul is still shocked the Galatian believers might choose to keep the law at the insistence of the agitators (5:7-10). Paul is confident his readers will agree with him rather than the rhetorical skills of the agitators. Using a sports metaphor, Paul asks the Galatians, who "cut in on you?" When a runner cuts off another during the race it is bad sportsmanship, even cheating. Paul is highlighting unfairness with this metaphor. The agitators have not "played fair" by not fully explaining what is at stake in accepting one part of the law.

Unfair Play

This unfair play is an allusion to the rhetorical skills of the agitators. They have used unfair persuasion to convince the Gentile believers of something which is not the whole truth. Paul's confidence is based on both his revelation from God and his argument from Scripture. Paul's preaching was accompanied by the work of the Holy Spirit rather than rhetorical polish. This is not to say Paul's preaching was bland. But rather than using flattery or other rhetorical subtleties a Greek orator might employ, Paul relied on the power of the Holy Spirit. More importantly, the ultimate source of Paul's preaching is direct revelation from God, not just a well-designed argument.

Paul quotes a proverb about a little leaven effecting the whole batch. This was probably a common saying analogous to "one bad apple spoils the whole bushel." The argument of the agitators may only have a small flaw, but that single flaw is enough to destroy the entire argument. The flaw is that their rhetoric is not from God, nor is their preaching accompanied by the power of the Holy Spirit. Paul is citing the higher authority, God (who gave him a direct revelation) and the Holy Spirit (who empowered his preaching of the gospel). If the agitators claimed to be from Jerusalem, Paul is claiming to represent God himself.

Persecution as Proof of Truth

Paul presents the persecution he faces as evidence he is teaching something quite different from the agitators (5:11). Prior to his encounter with Jesus, Paul would have agreed with his opponents. In fact, Paul was persecuting other Jews for preaching the message God raised Jesus from the dead. Some scholars argue that early in his ministry Paul taught Gentile converts to be circumcised but at some point later changed his mind. This change in practice was in order to realize more success among the Gentiles.

But this does not seem to be possible since Paul has already claimed in this letter that he did ministry among the Gentiles immediately after his conversion (in Arabia, Gal 1:17). After his experience on the road to Damascus, Paul believed Gentiles were being saved without converting to Judaism and keeping law.

While it is possible there were some years before he fully worked out the implications of Jesus as Messiah, he was persecuted almost immediately. Paul's preaching was offensive to the Jews because he claims Israel crucified their Messiah. The proof Jesus is the Messiah is that God raised him from the dead. For that reason alone Paul may have been persecuted by the Jerusalem hierarchy, as they did Peter and John (Acts 4–5) and Stephen (Acts 6–7).

But Paul may also refer to persecution from Jews in the synagogues of the Diaspora, who were offended by a gospel which allowed Gentiles to be a part of God's people apart from the law. In 2 Corinthians 6:4–5 Paul says he has been beaten and imprisoned. In 2 Corinthians 11:24 he claims he had been lashed by the Jews on five separate occasions. While Luke does not record these beatings in the book of Acts, there is no reason to think Paul did not encounter dangers as a result of his gospel from the very beginning of his ministry.

CONCLUSION

Paul's frustration overflows in a strong condemnation in 5:12. He is angered his churches would consider defecting to "another gospel" and he is upset the agitators are able to persuade the Gentiles in his churches to try to keep the law instead of standing firm in the freedom they have in Jesus. But like a college freshman, the Gentiles struggle with their freedom and they long for a return to the old rules in order to control their sinful passions. Even though they are free from the law, the Galatians still struggle to walk by the Spirit.

QUESTIONS FOR FURTHER DISCUSSION

1. What is the attraction of legalism today?
2. In what ways can legalism hinder spiritual growth, both for an individual and for a church?
3. How can persecution be an indication of the truth? What does this imply for Christians who never suffer for their faith?
4. To what extent does "a little leaven destroys the whole batch" apply to legalism in the local church?

13

Life in the Spirit
Galatians 5:13–26

INTRODUCTION

GALATIANS 5:13–26 IS A well-known text featuring the often-memorized "fruit of the Spirit." But for Paul this section of his letter answers the question of what a Christian community "looks like." The Gentile converts to Christ have left their traditional religious and social practices and want to know what defines "being in Christ." The agitators argue the Gentiles ought to keep the Jewish Law, implying the Gentiles have only partially converted when they accepted Paul's gospel. Paul has passionately argued against this: Gentiles are not converting to Judaism. They have become part of something new and different where the old social distinctions no longer matter. There is neither Jew nor Gentile in the body of Christ (3:26–29). In the present age there is equality in Christ coming from the Holy Spirit rather than from ethnicity or social standing. This means, Paul insists, the one who is "in Christ" is no longer under the Law.

This freedom in Christ is not the freedom to do whatever one pleases, nor is it a freedom to sin. When Paul talks about freedom in Christ he does not have in mind the modern libertarian sense of freedom as free from the restraints of law and morality. The believer in Christ is set free from the law, but this allows the believer to serve God. As he explains in Romans 6, we are free in Christ to be re-enslaved to a new master, God.

FREEDOM IN CHRIST (5:13-16)

The fact the believer is free from the law should not necessarily lead to the view that the believer may indulge in sinful behavior (5:13). Does Paul contradict himself in this verse? He has argued in this letter the believer is free from slavery to the law, but now he says the believer ought to resubmit to slavery, this time to his neighbor. Freedom from law is not a freedom from everything. We will always have some sort of obligation to fulfill, at least to the government and to our family. Paul has in mind our obligation to serve God by serving one another.

Still a Slave?

Since the one who is in Christ is free from the obligations of the law, they now must voluntarily re-enslave themselves to the Spirit. For Paul, there are only two possibilities: either one is enslaved to the flesh or one is enslaved to the Spirit. Paul will unpack what he means by flesh and Spirit in the next paragraph, but for now it is important to understand these are the only two options for the one who is in Christ.

Based on what Paul says in Galatians, the law is not an option for living out a life "in Christ." Nor is it acceptable to blend a life "in Christ" with something else, such as a Greek philosophy or worship of another god. Paul would be just as critical of the Galatian churches if they chose to live out a new life in Christ through popular Stoic or Epicurean ethical philosophy as he is with the Gentiles trying to keep the law.

Indulging the Sinful Nature

The fact we are free from the Mosaic law is not to be used as a reason to indulge in sinful behavior. The noun here refers to a starting point, like capital for a business venture or a military base from which an assault is launched. By the first century, the word was used for "pretext" or "occasion, opportunity." In 1 Timothy 5:14 it is used for an "excuse" for Satan to slander unmarried widows because of their moral lapses.

Since the believer in Christ is free from the Mosaic law, it is possible some people took Paul's gospel as a license to sin. Paul must deal with this problem here and in Romans 6:1–14 because people did take their freedom too far. Some of the problems described in 1 Timothy and Titus are a result of people "sinning so that grace might abound." The letter of Jude deals with people who "pervert the grace of our God into a license to sin" (Jude 4). If someone is free from all restraint of the law, what keeps them from indulging in all sorts of sin?

This is a common criticism of a Calvinist view of salvation. Someone might say, "If election and preservation means I cannot lose my salvation, then I can behave any way I would like and still be saved." The problem is neither Paul nor Calvin would agree with this sort of thinking. This is an issue of spiritual maturity. For example, imagine the first taste of freedom a teen has when they go to college. Mom and Dad are not watching them all of the time so they have the freedom to do whatever they want. As a result, many college freshmen get into trouble. While it is possible for a person to understand their freedom in Christ in this way, Paul says it is inappropriate for the one who is "walking by the Spirit" to indulge the sinful nature.

LOVE YOUR NEIGHBOR

Paul alludes to Leviticus 19:18: the law is fulfilled in one commandment, "Love your neighbor as yourself" (Gal 5:14). This verse is the most quoted verse from the Pentateuch in the New

Testament, despite the fact it is almost never referred to in first-century Jewish texts. Perhaps this is because Jesus himself stressed love of neighbor as a fulfillment of the law.

The Greatest Commandment

There was a lively debate in the first century on how to sum up the law. When a teacher of the law asks Jesus what the greatest command is, he responds, "to love the Lord your God with all your heart and your neighbor as yourself" (Matt 22:34–40). Jesus says the law and prophets "hang" on these two commandments.

However, defining just who was included as a neighbor was also a hotly debated topic. Prior to the parable of the Good Samaritan (Luke 10:25–37), Jesus is asked by an expert in the law to define "neighbor." The man likely understood the word "neighbor" to refer to his fellow Jews, since that is what it means in Leviticus. But Jesus expands "neighbor" to include anyone who is in need.

It is possible Paul has fellow Christians in mind here, given the context of factions within the church (5:15, 26), but he will expand the doing of good in 6:10 to everyone, but especially the "household of faith." Paul's point is not, "If you want to keep the law, love your neighbor." He has said repeatedly that the age of the law is done and over with and the one who is in Christ is free from the Mosaic law.

Free from Law, Free to Fulfill the Law

After arguing Gentiles do not have to keep the law, it is ironic Paul now says when they love their neighbors they "fulfill the law." It is as if Paul is saying, "If you really want to keep the law, love your neighbor." Like a prophet from the Old Testament, Paul tells his readers their observance of rituals does not mean anything if they do not do the heart of the law, namely, love of God and love of neighbors. If one is loving one's neighbor, then they are already doing the "spirit of the law." By walking by the Holy Spirit, the believer is already fulfilling the whole law.

Biting and Devouring

The reason the Galatian believers are to submit to the law of love in Christ is that their current behavior is going to destroy the church. They are biting and devouring one another (5:15). Paul describes the factions in the Galatian churches as wild animals. They are like "mad beasts fighting each other so that they went up killing each other."[1] Wild animals are commonly used as metaphors for bad behavior in the Greco-Roman world, so this is a metaphor the Galatians would have immediately understood.

There is a danger in keeping the law, but Paul says here there is also danger in factionalism. The body of Christ functions best when there is unity in local churches (Phil 2:1–4). The problem Paul must address is therefore, "How do I serve my brother and sister in love?" Paul answers this by contrasting "life in the flesh" and "life in the spirit."

WALKING BY FLESH (5:17–21)

Paul describes the conflict between flesh and Spirit (5:17–18). Is this struggle between the natural human inclination to do the right thing and the equally natural human inclination to do the wrong thing? Both Jewish and Greco-Roman ethical writing in the first century thought there was a struggle between a natural desire to do evil and the practice of virtue. For a Greek philosopher the problem was "animal passions"; for the Jewish thinkers the struggle was a result of sin. Paul describes the Christian experience as a new creation; old things have passed away (2 Cor 5:20). Those who are "in Christ" are people who are supposed to be led by the Holy Spirit and therefore should not be overcome by the vices Paul lists in the following verses.

---

1. Betz, *Galatians*, 277

Virtues and Vices

Three observations need to be made about vice and virtue lists. First, the key to understanding Paul's point is verse 16. The one who is led by the Spirit will not "gratify the desires of the flesh." The verb translated "gratify" is normally "complete." The one who is "in Christ" is able to overcome the fleshy desires and not "bring them to completion." Sin does not reign in the life of the believer; the Holy Spirit does.

Second, most of the vices listed in this section are in the plural. Paul is not talking about individual sins, but rather sins which typically affect the community as a whole. While it is certainly a problem when an individual commits these sins, Paul's concern is for the community of believers. A local church cannot survive when these sins are present.

Third, these lists are the result of being led by the flesh or led by the Holy Spirit. The verb in verse 18 is passive: the believer is being led with Holy Spirit as a guide. Paul contrasts this with being under the law, perhaps because the one who is still under the law is guided by the law and actively keeps that law. The one who is in Christ is yielded to the Holy Spirit as a guide rather than the law as a guardian. This is difficult for the believer because we would rather have a list of rules to actively follow rather than "being led" by the Holy Spirit.

Acts of the Sinful Nature

Even though he describes the "acts of the sinful nature" as obvious, Paul lists them anyway in 5:19–21. The list is broken up into two sections. The first describes the pagan world the Gentile converts in Galatia would have known well. These "pagan sins" frame the second list, which is the situation in the church at the moment. The sins in this list are all typically associated with meals at temples or pagan worship in general.

Bruce Winter gathers a number of references from Plutarch describing the combination of gluttony, drunkenness, and sexual

Life in the Spirit

immorality which were frequently a part of the Greco-Roman banquet.[2] There was an association between gluttony and sexual excess, as is seen from the well-known saying reported by Plutarch, "In well-gorged bodies love [passions] resides." Plutarch also said that "intemperate conversation follows a lawless meal, inharmonious music follows a shameless debauch." Attendance at these banquets was considered a social entitlement for young men. At eighteen, males were considered adults and had the right to wear a toga and to attend banquets. Winter cites several ancient writers warning young men of the dangers of attending the drunken debauchery at a banquet. It is possible many of the adult male members of the Galatian churches had at one time or another attended this kind of Greco-Roman banquet and knew exactly what Paul was talking about. Even if they had not attended themselves, everyone knew what went on during these celebrations.

Paul simply lists a series of "acts of the flesh" typical of Greco-Roman society. "Sexual immorality" covers a wide range of sexual sin, although most frequently it is associated with prostitution. Similarly, "impurity" has the connotation of uncleanliness associated with sexual sins. "Sensuality" refers to unbridled passion of sexual license.[3] This is the kind of activity which would have a Roman pagan blush! Both idolatry and sorcery were closely related and refer to pagan worship, including use of substances in order to receive visions. Drunkenness appears in the plural in verse 21 and refers to "regular bouts of drinking" which took place in Greco-Roman banquets. "Orgies" refers to excessive feasting, but was also used for the lewd procession of Dionysius.

The Church Cannot Live Like This

The list of "acts of the flesh" also includes a series of sins which are threatening to break apart the Christian community in Galatia. Witherington points out a contrast between these seven vices and

---

2. Winter, *After Paul Left Corinth*, 82–85.
3. Schreiner, *Galatians*, 346.

the fruit of the Spirit which follow.[4] There is hatred rather than love, discord rather than peace, anger rather than patience, rage rather than kindness, selfishness rather than generosity. By inserting this list into a description of rather obvious sins from the pagan world, Paul points out the shamefulness of hatred, discord, rage, etc. in the Galatian churches. Paul therefore envisions two ways of living as a community: one is self-centered and mean-spirited; the church is to be other-centered, community-spirited.

Paul says people who "live like this" will not inherit the kingdom of God (5:21). This cannot mean the Christian who has committed an act of immorality will lose their salvation. The person who "walks this way" is in danger of not obtaining an inheritance. Is "kingdom of God" used here as a description of "eternal life"? This is a possibility, although kingdom language like this usually refers to a future kingdom after the return of Jesus. It is possible Paul is alluding to the teaching of Jesus. In the Gospels a rich young man asks Jesus what he must do to "inherit eternal life" (Mark 10:17). In either case, Paul says these acts of the sinful nature will kill the church if they are allowed to continue.

WALKING BY SPIRIT (5:22-26)

In contrast to the acts of the sinful nature, Paul describes the "fruit of the Spirit," a virtue list which describes how the believer will walk. As observed above, the fruit of the Spirit are community-oriented characteristics. A community of believers walking in the Spirit will be characterized by this fruit.

Virtue as "Fruit"

That Paul uses the metaphor of fruit is important. If the church is a new creation, they will grow and they will bear fruit. These characteristics will naturally be present in the church, as opposed to the "works of the flesh." A tree by its nature bears fruit, and you

---

4. Witherington, *Grace in Galatia*, 402.

can tell what kind of tree it is by the fruit it bears. If a tree does not bear any fruit at all, then something is wrong with the tree. It is unhealthy and something needs to be done to fix the problem preventing the tree from bearing fruit.

It is also important that Paul calls this list the "fruit of the Spirit," not the "fruits." Sometimes this is taken to mean the believer is responsible for all of the fruit of the Spirit, in contrast to receiving only a few of the "gifts of the Spirit." This is possible, but Paul rarely uses the word "fruit" in the plural. In Ephesians 5:9, for example, the "fruit of light" refers to "all that is good, right, and true" in contrast to unfruitful "acts of darkness."

The singular word for fruit does highlight the cumulative effect of all nine of the virtues listed here.[5] One cannot claim to be walking by the Spirit and practicing peace, for example, while not practicing gentleness or kindness. Everything Paul lists here works together as a way of "walking by the Spirit." All believers are encouraged to bear all the fruit at all times. One cannot say "patience is not my fruit" and therefore ignore patience as a virtue. If a person is walking by the Holy Spirit, then all of the fruit will be evident in their life.

The last three of the fruit are also Greek virtues, and the final line ("against such there is no law") may be an allusion to the ethical teaching of Aristotle.[6] Paul's point is that a Spirit-led Christian not only fulfills the heart of the Mosaic law but will be considered virtuous in a Greco-Roman sense as well. The Spirit-led life is therefore the best of both the Mosaic law and the ethics of the philosophers. If a Christian is living a life characterized by love, peace, patience, etc., they will be respected even by the pagans!

The fruit are fairly easy to define and can be related to the life and character of Jesus. James Dunn calls this list a "character sketch of Jesus."[7] Since the believer has the Holy Spirit, Paul's ethical command is simple: keep in step with the Spirit, not the flesh. This is another example of Paul telling the Galatians to be

---

5. Moo, *Galatians*, 366.
6. Witherington, *Grace in Galatia*, 407.
7. Dunn, *Galatians*, 310.

"in Christ" without giving them a series of commands to follow or steps to accomplish.

THE FRUIT OF THE SPIRIT (5:22-23)

In contrast to the "obvious" works of the flesh, Paul offers a list of virtues characterizing the one who is walking by the Spirit. Like the works of the flesh, this is not a complete list of every virtue. Paul has several other lists of virtues that include some of these seven and add many others. For example, in Ephesians 4:1-3 Paul refers to humility, patience, love, unity, and peace.

Love

It is possible Paul places this virtue first in the list because it is the foundation for all virtue. 1 Corinthians 13 says "without love you can do nothing" and the greatest virtue is love. Modern culture has unfortunately equated love with romance, making it difficult to appreciate what is meant by the word in the Bible. Romans 5:6-8 gives the best illustration of love from a biblical perspective: when we were still sinners God demonstrated his love for us by sending his son to die on the cross on our behalf. The love Paul has in mind is not sentimental human love, but rather the kind of love coming from God through the Holy Spirit.

Paul begins with love since the practice of love will create unity, which is currently lacking in the Galatian churches. In Colossians 2:2 Paul says love will "knit together" the hearts of believers. In the modern use of the word, love is sometimes a nebulous feeling one has, but in Paul's view love results in concrete actions. Just a few verses earlier in Galatians Paul stated the believer is free in Christ to serve other believers in love (cf. Rom 14:15).

Like all of the fruit, love is a characteristic of God. In fact, 1 John 4:4:7-8 states, "God is love." In Hosea 11 God describes his love for Israel as a deep, unimaginable compassion for his children. In Hosea 2:14-15 God describes his love for Israel as the tender love of a young married couple. God will "allure" his people and speak tenderly to Israel: "I will betroth you in righteousness and justice, in love and compassion." The practice of love in a Christian community is therefore an expression of the character of God.

Joy

Greco-Roman descriptions of joy emphasize pleasure, exhilaration, or excitement. In contrast, Paul uses the word in a way which has little to do with circumstances. Joy looks at present circumstances through the lens of our hope of salvation (Rom 5:2). In Philippians Paul repeats the phrase "rejoice in the Lord" despite the fact he is in prison and does not know if he will be released. In fact, Paul says he is "being poured out like a drink offering" (Phil 2:17) yet still rejoices in the Lord!

For the one who is walking by the Spirit, circumstances have little to do with happiness. This is not to say one must be happy about suffering hard times. Since we have a hope in Jesus which gives context to that suffering, we can rise above the circumstance and have a true joy.

Peace

Peace is not usually listed in the New Testament as a virtue. In fact, it is rarely thought of as something one "does." Paul sometimes says we have "peace with God" (Rom 5:1-2; Eph 2:17), but the word can also describe our relationship with other people. Paul's understanding of peace should be grounded in the Hebrew idea of *shalom* rather than the Greek idea of serenity or quietness. *Shalom* is the sense things are the way they should be. This kind of peace can be described as wholeness, soundness, or even prosperity. True peace naturally produces unity (Eph 4:3), the very thing with which the Galatian believers are struggling.

Peace could refer to peace with God (Rom 5:1) or peace with other people (Eph 2:14-18). The one who is walking by the Spirit already has peace with God. Once we were enemies of God, but now we are reconciled to God through the work of Jesus. But if we have been reconciled to God and are in a state of peace with him, there ought to be some sort of change in our relationships with other people. The one who is walking by the Spirit ought to be a peacemaker, someone who promotes an environment of peace. Imagine how different a church would be if everyone actively sought to live in peace with one another.

Patience

Patience is one of the chief characteristics of God in the Old Testament. God is patient, literally having "long temper" or being "longsuffering." Exodus 34:6 describes God as "slow to anger" and compassionate. Just as God was patient with his people in the Old Testament, Jesus was patient with his disciples. There are many stories in the Old Testament where God gives his people opportunity to repent and return to covenant faithfulness. The primary example of God's patience is Adam and Eve. When they rebel against God's command he offers them both mercy and grace by covering their shame and giving them long lives.

What does it mean to be patient with other people? One of the best examples of a patient person is a kindergarten teacher. A person who teaches very young children has to be slow to anger, giving them a long time to learn lessons. Perhaps there is need for some correction, but even correction is given in a positive way so the children will continue to grow and develop. Imagine a crusty old army sergeant teaching a classroom full of squirrely kindergarten boys. How long would his patience last? The one who is walking by the Spirit is patient with everyone because they have experienced God's patience in the past.

Kindness and Goodness

Kindness and goodness are very close in meaning and are related to mercy and grace. Kindness is generosity and showing compassion to those who are in need; goodness is the attitude which prompts a person to do acts of kindness.

Like patience, kindness is a characteristic of God; perhaps both words are related to God's lovingkindness (*hesed*) in the Old Testament. Lovingkindness is illustrated in Ruth's loyalty towards Naomi, but the word appears often to describe the character of God. God is ultimately loyal to his people despite their utter disloyalty. In Romans 2:4 Paul says God extends a gracious kindness to the sinful world by allowing the world time to repent. Rather than giving humanity what they deserve, God is generous in his mercy and allows sinners time to repent.

Faithfulness

Faithfulness is also rooted in the character of God. Rather than "having faith," this word emphasizes keeping one's promises. God "abounds in faithfulness" (Exod 34:6) and his "steadfast love" can never cease (Ps 77:8; 107:1). The one who is walking by the Spirit will be faithful to their word and loyal to their commitments both to God and other people.

Gentleness

Gentleness is an often misunderstood virtue since it is sometimes translated "meekness," giving the impression a gentle person is weak and easily manipulated. But in Greek ethics this word referred to the "golden mean" between being too angry and being unable to get angry. Essentially, the gentle person is in control of their emotions at all times.

Self-Control

This final fruit of the Spirit was one of the most important Greek ethical terms. Remarkably, the Greek world valued controlling one's passions and acting moderately in all things. Any activity could devolve into a vice if it is not practiced with moderation. For example, eating a proper amount of food is a good thing; too much is glutton and too little is starvation. Paul claims here the one who is walking by the Spirit will walk moderately in everything they do. In fact, Paul points out the person who belongs to Christ Jesus has "crucified the flesh with its passions and desires."

"Against Such There Is No Law"

The final line in verse 23 can be taken several ways. It may be as simple as, "There are no laws in any culture against these virtues." It is unimaginable any culture would make "kindness and gentleness" against the law. But in parallel with the final line of the "works of the flesh," the line might mean the person who is "walking in the Spirit" as demonstrated by this fruit will avoid the curse of the law (Gal 3:10).

It is important to remember the agitators in Galatia are telling the Gentile converts they must keep the law in order to be right with God. Paul argues throughout the letter the Gentiles are not converting to Judaism and they are therefore not under the Mosaic covenant. But Paul does not release Gentiles from all moral responsibility. The one who is walking by the Spirit of God, Paul says, will naturally produce the fruit of the Spirit. Rather than following a set of proscribed rules and regulations, believers are to produce the fruit they were designed to bear as the "in Christ" people of God.

Paul does not give any sort of description of how this takes place. There is no "seven laws of the fruitful Christian." Nor does he provide a series of commands guaranteeing the result of love, joy, and peace. He simply says, "Walk in step with the Spirit." Perhaps this is more frustrating than keeping the law!

KEEP ON WALKING

Paul returns to the problem of factions in the concluding line of the chapter. If the believer is walking in the Spirit and producing the fruit of the Spirit, then there is no room for conceit or envy, the very things causing factions within the Galatian churches. The metaphor "keeping in step with the Spirit" (v. 24) has the sense of following a leader in a line, or like soldiers moving in formation. Picture a formal military parade: all of the solders act as a single unit and follow precisely the commands called out by their leader. The result of "walking with the Spirit" is the whole church acting as a unified whole in order to do the will of the Spirit.

If the church is walking in step with the Spirit, they will not be conceited, leading to provocations and jealousy (v. 26). The word usually translated "conceited" has the sense of being "falsely proud." It is one thing to boast in something that is real and true, but this word refers to boasting in something that is not actually real. In the context of Galatians, the agitators have a false self-confidence before God because they are basing their justification on their law-keeping rather than "walking in the Spirit."

CONCLUSION

The contrast between the "acts of the flesh" and the "fruit of the Spirit" is very clear. Rather than present a revised version of the Old Testament law, Paul describes what a person who is in Christ looks like. It is easy to understand the acts of the flesh, but it is difficult to imagine all the implications of the fruit of the Sprit. Rather than offer us a list of commands to follow, Paul simply states the principles and allows the believer to apply the fruit of the Spirit to various moral choices. How can we be loving in a world filled with hatred? How can we be agents of peace in a world filled with rage and malice?

The problem for modern Christians is we enjoy pointing out sins in other people while failing to yield to the Holy Spirit in order to develop our sensitivity to the application of the fruit of the Spirit in our own lives.

QUESTIONS FOR FURTHER DISCUSSION

1. Jesus also said the law could be summarized by loving God with your whole heart and loving your neighbor as yourself. How does Paul differ from this common Jewish view of the law?
2. How can implementing the fruit of the Spirit result in unity within the church?
3. What are some specific ways the church can practice the fruit of the Spirit?
4. Paul says if a believer is walking in step with the Spirit they will win the respect of outsiders. Can you give examples of this principle from your own experience? Are there examples of not "walking by the Spirit" which resulted in a loss of respect?

14

Doing Good to All
Galatians 6:1–10

INTRODUCTION

IN THIS LETTER, PAUL has argued Gentiles are not under the law. Gentiles do not need to keep the Jewish law since the purpose for that law has already been fulfilled in Christ's death on the cross. Rather than slaves to the law, the Galatian believers are God's adopted children (4:1–7). As such, they ought to behave as members of God's family. In the previous section of the letter Paul outlined what this new family looks like: avoiding the works of the flesh and developing the fruit of the Spirit.

There may have been some readers who thought Paul's view of freedom in Christ meant they no longer had any obligation to help members of the church or even members of their own family. There is a contrast between bearing the burden of the law and bearing one another's burdens. These burdens may be spiritual, but there are real physical burdens in mind here as well. The household of God is called to do good to all people, beginning with those in the household who cannot carry their own burdens.

RESTORING OTHERS GENTLY (6:1)

Those who live by the Spirit will restore one another when they are "caught in sin." What does this mean? To be "caught in sin" sounds like a person has been caught "red-handed" in the act of a sin. Sometimes people think that if they are not caught a sin does not count against them. Most people drive cars as if speed limits are general suggestions and they are not doing anything wrong unless they get caught. The word Paul uses here is usually translated "overtake," as in hunting down an animal. A person who has been caught in sin has been ensnared or trapped and they are in need of rescue.

If a person is caught in sin, they are to be restored, or "returned to their former condition." The verb is used in Matthew 4:21 with reference to mending fishing nets. This kind of restoration is to be done "gently," the same word used in the fruit of the Spirit in Galatians 5:23. This means the church is not to be arrogant or inconsiderate when dealing with a public sin. A church ought to seek to restore a person to fellowship without humiliating the person who was caught by a sin.

Restoration to Fellowship

In this verse, the goal of any correction is a restoration of the brother who has sinned. Paul is not creating an inquisition looking for potential sin to investigate church members. But Paul does warn the reader not to think too much of themselves. His main concern is conceit. Like Galatians 5:26, Paul is concerned the one who "walks by the Spirit" will be tempted, perhaps thinking they are spiritually mature when they are not. Paul is concerned people will deceive themselves into thinking they are so spiritually mature they are free from the same dangers as the one who was caught.

On the other hand, helping another believer deal with their own burden of sin can lead to a superior attitude toward the person caught in sin. Once a person starts thinking they are superior, they might start condemning others in inappropriate ways. There is a fine balance between confronting a brother or sister in Christ who has a problem and meddling in things which are not your business.

Examine Yourself

Self-examination is critical for a community of believers. While Paul has encouraged restoring a brother caught in sin, he is not inviting the congregation to investigate the private lives of other members of the congregation. On the contrary, the first (and only) person believers ought to investigate is themselves.

In 6:1 Paul says the spiritual ones who are trying to restore a person caught in sin ought to examine themselves first. In 6:4 he says each believer ought to test their own work. Both words have the sense of critical examination. For example, think of this examination as similar to a tax audit. During the audit an accountant carefully goes over every financial transaction in order to confirm everything is as is it ought to be. Most Christians do not think about examining their own hearts that diligently.

Paul is concerned those who have to deal with sin will themselves be caught in sin. While this might refer to being tempted by the same sin the first person was caught in, Paul is concerned they themselves will be caught in the sin of conceit. Humble self-examination is the only antidote to conceited arrogance.

BEAR ONE ANOTHER'S BURDENS (6:2-5)

In the context of verse 1, this "bearing a burden" may refer to a burden carried by the brother or sister caught in sin. But the language could also refer to financial burdens. This is possible since the next paragraph deals with helping others financially. There is a great deal in this paragraph to indicate Paul has financial burdens in mind, although it is not appropriate to limit the "burdens" to only financial distress.

The warning in verse 3 is significant since it implies persons who are not willing to help other believers carry their burden deceive themselves by thinking they are "something." Perhaps some might think they are too important to help the poorer members of the congregation. In the Greco-Roman world, the more elite and honored a person was, the less likely they would be to help anyone beneath them socially.

The ideal situation for Paul is that everyone takes care of their own "load" (v. 5). This word can refer to a ship's cargo (Acts 27:10). Elsewhere Paul says people ought to work hard to provide for their needs rather than relying on the church to meet their own needs (1 Thess 4:11–12; 2 Thess 3:12; Eph 4:28). But there are times when members of the family of God find themselves in difficult circumstances. Paul considers this a "family matter" and the family ought to look out for members who are in need.

THE LAW OF CHRIST

By bearing one another's burdens, the believer "fulfills the law of Christ" (v. 4). What is the "law of Christ"? One possibility is the law of Christ is at least a portion of the Mosaic law, perhaps the moral aspects of the law. It is hard to believe, however, that Paul would say the Gentile believers in Galatia could do part of the law by helping those who struggle with sin.

A second possibility is that this refers to the teachings of Jesus in the Gospels. This is attractive since Paul taught the churches in Galatia about the life, death, and resurrection of Jesus. But it is hard to point to a passsage in the Gospels, which were written after Galatians, such as the Greatest Commandment (Matt 22:34–40), as "the law of Christ."

A third way to understand the "law of Christ" is as a contrast to the law of Moses. Romans 3:21–26 makes this point by contrasting the law of works (the Mosaic law) with the righteousness obtained through the death of Jesus. In this view, the law of Christ is equivalent to the new covenant (1 Cor 11:23–26), the law of the Spirit (Rom 8:2), and walking by the Spirit (Gal 5:22–23).

Doing Good to All

To "fulfill" this law is to carry out a responsibility or obligation. The word occasionally means "to complete a work." Members of the Galatian churches wanted to fulfill the law of Moses, yet they could never actually keep the whole law, let alone "complete it." Paul now tells them they can fully complete the law of Christ by bearing the burdens of their brothers and sisters.

REAPING AND SOWING (6:6-8)

Several times in his letters Paul tells his congregations to support their teachers. In 1 Corinthians 9:3-14, for example, he uses an analogy from the law to argue the one who labors is worthy of being paid. He uses the same metaphor of sowing and reaping several times in that context. In the Greek text, the first word in Galatians 6:6 is "share." This word has the sense of partnership, as in Philippians 4:15. One can share in good things, such as spiritual blessings (Rom 15:27), or in sin (1 Tim 5:22). Paul used the same word in Romans 12:13 to refer to "contributing to the needs of the saints."

The one who is instructed and the instructor are not words normally associated with pastors and teachers in the Pauline letters. The word is sometimes associated with catechism, since the English comes from this Greek word. Luke used the word in Luke 1:4, where Theophilus has been taught certain things about Jesus. It is also used to describe Apollos as a well-educated disciple (Acts 18:25). James uses the same word to describe the report that Paul was (allegedly) teaching Jews to forsake the law (Acts 21:21, 24).

Supporting Pastors and Teachers

How were teachers in the earliest church supported? Was this a problem Paul has to address? Were the Galatian churches not supporting their teachers?

Paul's point becomes clearer as the passage develops. The churches in Galatia were already collecting support for those in need in order to help "bear burdens" (v. 2). It may be the case churches overlooked the needs of those who were laboring on behalf of the church. Paul has already told them to support members of the congregation who have genuine needs and he will tell them to do good to all people in verse 10. Paul inserts this reminder to care for those who are working in the church as well.

Paul warns his readers God is not mocked. The verb translated "mocked" means to "turn one's nose up" at something. This is to treat something with contempt. The only other place in the New Testament the word appears is Luke 23:35, where it is used to describe how people treated Jesus while he hung on the cross: "they scoffed at him." In Psalm 80:6 the enemies laugh at God's people because they are under his punishment. In Jeremiah 20:7 it is used for "made a laughingstock." Ben Witherington points out that mocking one's opponents was a regular practice for Greco-Roman orators.[1] If this sort of mockery and jeering was a part of public discourse, Paul's point is God will not be affected by it.

Reaping and Sowing

Paul uses a metaphor people in the ancient world would clearly understand. Someone who sows seed expects to reap a harvest from the seed (6:8). It is possible the source for this metaphor is Proverbs 22:7–9, but the concept of sowing and reaping is common in both Greek and Roman writers as well. There is no question Paul is talking about giving in this passage, giving to help the burdens of others and to support teachers in local churches. But what does Paul mean by "reaping" in this context?

Verse 8 contrasts sowing to the flesh as opposed to sowing to the Spirit. Paul has already used this sort of contrast in Galatians 5:16, although there it was walking by the flesh or walking by the Spirit. Now Paul draws a contrast with self-centered actions, whether circumcision (the theme of the letter) or any other act motivated out of a desire to benefit oneself. In contrast, "sowing to

---

1. Witherington, *Grace in Galatia*, 431

the Spirit" are the outward acts motivated by a desire to do good in the church and in the community.

The "harvest" will be either "corruption" or "eternal life." On the surface, this sounds like Paul is telling the readers if they are doing good works they get to go to heaven when they die, as opposed to hell. But in the context of Galatians this seems unlikely. One is made righteous through faith, not works (2:16–21). The verb "harvest" is in the future tense, implying they will receive the harvest in the future. Perhaps the future aspect of harvesting is necessary for the metaphor: farmers first sow their fields and then at a later time they reap.

The metaphor of sowing and reaping appears often in the context of future judgment in the Gospels. In Matthew 13:24–30, when Jesus returns it will be like a harvest. He will separate the wheat from the weeds and put the wheat where it belongs (in the barn) and the weeds where they belong (on the fire). Paul is talking about a judgment believers will face when they stand before the judgment seat of Christ. Some things which we have sown in this life will yield a crop worthy of reward; others actions will yield a worthless crop which will be burned (1 Cor 3:10–15).

Unfortunately "sowing and reaping" has been taken out of context to claim God will only bless those who give enough money to the right ministry, or buy books from the right authors. Paul is not saying if you give to your local church you will personally reap a harvest of prosperity in this life. Our acts of selfless service are no longer selfless if we expect to receive a reward. The reward for sharing without brothers and sisters in need will be given at the future judgment seat of Christ.

LET US DO GOOD TO ALL (6:9–10)

If the one who is walking in the Spirit is supporting the local Christian community, how was that community supposed to use the support? "Doing good" might refer to doing things which were considered civic virtue in the community. For a Greek or Roman, to "do good" meant donating money to some civic improvement or paying for a sacrifice honoring a dead ancestor. Rarely would a Roman consider how their good deed helped "all people." The only reason to do a good deed was to gain more honor and prestige for themselves.

In a Jewish context "doing good" might refer to giving to the poor, protecting the widow and orphan, and even burying the dead. Since the theme of giving money is prominent in this chapter, it is possible Paul's command here was applied to a community fund which was collected and distributed to those in need. If the Galatian churches were made of people from various social strata, then some of the members might have had real physical needs while others had the means to meet those needs.

Growing Weary of Doing Good

Paul warns his readers not to become weary in doing these acts of goodness. The phrase appears in 2 Thessalonians 3:13. The word Paul uses here sometimes refers to discouragement, or losing heart, perhaps even being afraid. The final phrase uses another verb which refers to being exhausted or worn out. It appears in several military contexts to indicate losing one's nerve. Why would someone become discouraged or afraid of doing good deeds?

One option is a lack of response from those who are helped. To extend the sowing and reaping metaphor, if a farmer sowed seed in a field and nothing ever grew, he might give up sowing that particular field. There are many Christians who do "thankless jobs." If you volunteer at a homeless shelter, you can do many good things for people but there might be little or no response from the people you are trying to help. This lack of a response is very discouraging.

A second option is someone in Paul's churches was afraid to do good works such as helping the poor in a community because helping the poor was not considered to be a virtue. A social elite in one of the Galatian churches may not see in any benefit to their personal honor by helping the poor slaves who were also in the church. Later in history, Christians often helped people who were very sick, even when their own lives were a risk. It is possible this is a real fear people felt when doing acts of mercy.

A third option is people who are busy doing good things often do get tired of the work. Paul may very well have in mind physical exhaustion from serving people in the community. This is a danger in any kind of service, but it if someone is serving in a ministry where they are working hard and never see any results, they naturally become exhausted and discouraged.

The fact Paul includes a condition in verse 9, "if we do not give up," is an indication the harvest or reward does not happen automatically. It is hard work to be a member of God's family, but it is ultimately rewarding.

Doing good begins with the "household of faith" and moves outward to everyone else. This may be people in need within the family of God because they have a burden they cannot bear. It also includes those who have been called by God to teach the Scripture in the local church.

CONCLUSION

If the Christian is walking in step with the Holy Spirit, then they will naturally seek to do good toward others. The challenge of this passage is keeping our giving Christ-centered. It is very easy to be motivated by our desire to be blessed by God, but his motivation is far from Paul's mind in Galatians 6. For Paul, the church is really a new family, and as a family we ought to care for one another's needs.

QUESTIONS FOR FURTHER DISCUSSION

1. What are some practical ways members of local churches can help bear the burdens of people in the church?
2. How has the principle of "reaping and sowing" (Gal 6:7–8) been abused in the modern church? Does this motivation for giving lead to self-centeredness?

3. How does Paul's "reaping and sowing" metaphor apply to the ways modern churches support their pastors and teachers?

4. What are some practical ways you can encourage those who serve in your local congregation?

15

Bearing the Marks of Jesus
Galatians 6:11–18

INTRODUCTION

I MUST CONFESS I am not a master preacher when it comes to concluding a sermon. Because my primary ministry is in the university classroom, I am used to ending at the time class is over (since students are likely to just get up and leave the room anyway). There have been a number of times when I have been preaching a sermon and I realized time had gotten away from me and I needed to conclude the sermon, but I was only just finishing my second of three points. (Isn't three the God-ordained number for sermon points?) Rather than rush through the last point or go longer than my assigned time, I chose to close in prayer. The closing prayer, however, became a summary sermon with most of my third point added in for good measure. After all, I had worked hard on the third point and I was going to get it in no matter what!

This is an example of "what not to do" when preaching a sermon, but for a letter writer in the first century, reviewing the letter and adding a few final encouragements was expected. Paul has already shown his independence from the Jerusalem church and the validity of his apostleship. He has made a clear scriptural argument showing the Gentiles they are not under the old covenant and should not submit to circumcision or attempt to keep the Jewish law. He has warned them of the dangers of going back to the law as well as shown them how to live out their freedom in Christ. Now in this final paragraph of the letter Paul will add a personal note summarizing the letter for the Galatian churches and remind them his call to freedom in Christ is a serious matter indeed.

WHAT BIG LETTERS! HOW PAUL WROTE LETTERS (6:11)

Beginning in 6:11, the words of the letter are written directly by Paul rather than working with a secretary. He specifically says this paragraph is "by his own hand." This is a normal procedure for a letter in the first century. A writer would dictate the letter to a professional scribe (amanuensis), who composed the letter using a style appropriate to the content. After the letter was finished, the writer may have worked with the secretary to edit the letter to ensure it reflected the intentions of the author. Depending on the needs of the writer, a secretary could have a considerable influence on how the letter was written.

After the writer was satisfied with the content of the letter, he often added a few words in his own handwriting in order to personalize the letter and to give approval to the contents. This is analogous to a political advertisement ending with the candidate saying "I approve of this message." Sometimes thank-you letters from a ministry have brief handwritten notes from the organization's president, often personalized to make the form letter feel friendlier.

In this case, Paul wrote in "large letters." It is likely Paul's handwriting differed from the scribe's so it was obvious another writer was finishing off the letter. But why "big letters"? One possibility is the phrase "big letters" refers to the whole of Galatians, so Paul is saying, "Look how long this letter is!" More likely, Paul is referring to the size of his handwriting in contrast to the professional scribe. Dunn suggests the letters were large enough for the reader to hold the letter up so the congregation could see Paul's own handwriting and read it for themselves.[1] Paul seems to have had some sort of eye problem while he was working in the Galatian churches (Gal 4:15), so it may be the case he wrote in large letters simply because he could not see well enough to write in normal letters. Although several other letters end with personal greetings from Paul, this is the only letter which mentions the "large letters."

Only the original copy of the letter would have had the large letters in Paul's handwriting. Since Galatians was sent to a number of churches in a region, it is likely the original letter was carried by Paul's representative. This person would read the letter from Paul and be available to answer any questions on behalf of Paul. The "signed letter" was the representative's letter of recommendation from Paul. We cannot know for sure, but it is likely a copy of the letter was made and left with the church and the representative carried the original on to the next church on his route.

Personal conclusions to Paul's letter were common and they normally included several things omitted in this letter. For example, Paul often includes some mention of his travel plans and a few prayer requests, but these are not found in Galatians. The introduction of the letter is missing Paul's usual prayer for the church, and the conclusion is missing personal greetings or a final prayer. While this is unusual, it is fitting with the nature of the letter. Paul was angry with the agitators who were trying to destroy his work among the Gentiles and frustrated with the members of his churches who were being swayed by the agitator's insistence on keeping the law.

As Dunn puts it, "with stylus firmly in hand"[2] Paul offers a summary and conclusion to the letter. He not only reminds his readers of his main points, but he also makes a final expression of his frustration with his opponents in Galatia.

---

1. Dunn, *Galatians*, 335.
2. Dunn, *Galatians*, 335.

GALATIANS

WHAT MOTIVATES THE OPPONENTS? (6:12-15)

Paul first points out the opponents are only interested in "making a good showing" in the flesh. The verb translated "make a good showing" concerns the pursuit of honor. This might be read as "they want to look good," but not in the sense of physical appearance. If they can convince the Gentile Christians to submit to circumcision and keep the law, they will appear to have honor in their community. Paul might be using a play on words here since circumcision is an act done to the flesh, and for the entire Greek and Roman world it was considered a mutilation of the flesh and an embarrassing dishonor. Only Jews would consider the rite an honor.

The second problem Paul has with his opponents is their desire to avoid persecution by forcing the Gentile believers to be circumcised. In 2 Corinthians 11 Paul argues his persecution for the cross of Christ is a proof his gospel is from God. Since he is suffering in ways similar to Jesus, he is living out his gospel with the humble service represented by Jesus (Phil 2:5-11).

In 2:3 Paul reminded his readers the Gentile Titus was not compelled to be circumcised. At least at the time of the first meeting between Paul and the Jerusalem church, there was an agreement Gentiles were not converting to Judaism and therefore were not required to keep the law. But something appears to have changed since the earlier meeting since some teachers from Jerusalem had targeted Paul's Gentile believers and tried to convince them to "fully convert" to be saved. The way Paul describes the situation here implies there was a possibility of persecution if these Gentile believers were not compelled to accept circumcision and the law. What changed? There are two major suggestions, although they are not mutually exclusive.

Jewish Nationalism?

Paul Jewett argued Jewish nationalism was on the rise in Judea in the mid-first century. If Paul's opponents were Jewish Christians, then perhaps they feared persecution from non-Christian Jews in Jerusalem and Judea who were beginning to be suspicious of the followers of Jesus.

As long as Christianity appeared to be a sect of loyal Jews who thought their teacher was the Messiah, then there was little problem. But once some Jesus-followers began to reach out to Gentiles and bring them into fellowship with Jews without proper conversion, then there was a danger to the very heart of Judaism. In Galatians Paul states unequivocally the age of the law has come to an end and that Christ-followers are new creations living in a new age of the Spirit. This would be very radical to the increasingly nationalistic Jews in Judea a decade before the first Jewish revolt.

Paul's persecution of Jewish Christians in Jerusalem and Damascus is an example of this very thing. Prior to his Damascus road experience, Paul thought the Jesus-followers were a dangerous threat to the heart of Judaism, although it was Stephen's attack on the temple and the ongoing claim the Messiah had been executed by the high priest which was Paul's motivation.

Fear of Persecution?

On the other hand, Bruce Winter suggested the opponents were motivated by a fear of persecution from the Romans. The Jewish religion was given a special exemption from participation in the imperial cult. The temple made sacrifices to the God of Israel on behalf of the emperor and that was considered to be their act of loyalty. Jews were therefore not required to participate in the imperial cult. Prior to Paul's mission, Jews were an ethnic minority living throughout the empire and clearly distinct from their Gentile neighbors.

But as Paul's gospel began to make progress among the Gentiles and these Gentiles were not required to convert to Judaism, it is possible the Gentile converts could become targets of Rome for withdrawing from the imperial cult. In this case, the motivation for compelling the Gentiles to fully submit to the law was to make them appear to be fully Jewish and therefore exempt from the imperial cult. If local Roman officials took notice of too many Gentiles claiming a Jewish exemption, it is possible both Jews and Christians could face penalties and persecution.

A problem with this view is Rome did not persecute the Jews in an organized way anywhere in the empire. But this is a fear a possible persecution. Diaspora Jews living in Gentile cities tended to keep a low profile so as not to invite persecution as "strangers and aliens" with strange practices.

Whatever the source of persecution, the opponents of Paul sought to convert the Gentile Christians to a form of Judaism to avoid persecution, either their own at the hands of other Jews or from Roman civil officials who were suspicious of anyone who did not participate in the imperial cult.

LIVING IN THE WRONG AGE

The third problem Paul highlights is the opponent's desire to remain in the previous age rather than live as new creations in Christ Jesus. This is the most dangerous element of the opponent's agenda and is clearly addressed throughout the letter.

For Paul, in this new age of grace ritual circumcision counts for nothing. It is a sign of a covenant which is no longer in effect. The old covenant has been replaced by the new and the Holy Spirit is the sign of participation in that new covenant. It is more than inappropriate to live under the old covenant. For Paul, to go back to the law runs the risk of nullifying the grace of God and renders the cross of Christ pointless (2:15–21).

In contrast to the motivations of the opponents, Paul will only boast in the cross of Jesus (6:14). Since he met Jesus on the Damascus road, Paul considers the whole world as "crucified." By this he means there is nothing in this world Paul counts as more important than the gospel of Jesus Christ.

THE RULE (6:16–18)

Having concluding his final argument against the opponents, Paul now pronounces a very Jewish blessing on the readers to the letter. The words "peace and mercy" are drawn from the Old Testament and were common in Jewish benedictions in the first century. It may see odd for Paul to vigorously argue against a central boundary marker in Judaism then conclude the letter with a typical Jewish blessing.

The blessing of peace and mercy is on those who live by "this rule." The Greek word Paul chose refers to a standard for judgment and can refer to a measuring stick. You know something is three feet long because you compare it to a yardstick, a standard for judging length. In this case, the "standard" Paul has in mind is verse 15: only a new life in Christ counts in the present age of grace.

Israel of God

The phrase "Israel of God" in 6:16 is one of the more difficult problems in Galatians. The phrase has been understood as a reference to the church as a new Israel, but this would seem to run counter to the argument of the whole letter. Paul's point is the church is neither Jewish nor Gentile. Since he has argued consistently through the letter that Gentiles are not converting to Judaism, it would be very strange to call the church a "new Israel" in the final lines of the book.

Many commentators think Paul is referring to his Jewish Christian opponents as the "Israel of God." In this case, the blessing is on "Christians who follow Paul's rule" with respect to the law and also on Christians who disagree with Paul, including the opponents who have harassed Paul in Galatia. Paul is making a final appeal for agreement on the topic of Gentile conversion.

Finally, it is possible "Israel of God" refers to non-Christian Jewish people. If this is the case, then Paul's blessing is on both Christians and Jews.

Paul's final word on this matter is to ask his opponents to stop causing him trouble on this matter. He used the same word for trouble in 2 Corinthians 6:5 and 11:23 with the sense of physical persecution. In that context Paul is listing the hardships and beatings he had endured for the sake of the gospel.

BEARING THE MARKS OF JESUS

Paul does not expect any more trouble with his opponents because he already "bears the marks of Jesus" (6:17). Like "Israel of God," this phrase has generated a great deal of discussion. The noun Paul chose to use refers to branding, but the exact sense of the metaphor is unclear. First, Paul could be referring to the practice of branding slaves. If this is the case, then Paul is describing himself as a "slave of Jesus" (cf. Phil 1:1). Second, the practice of tattooing one's body to honor a particular god was common in the ancient world. While this is an intriguing possibility, there is no other place in Paul's letters using this metaphor.

The most common suggestion is the "marks" are real physical scars Paul has resulting from his persecutions. Based on 2 Corinthians 11, Paul was beaten in the synagogue on five occasions and by the Romans on three others. Just prior to the writing of the letter to the Galatians, Paul was stoned and left for dead at Lystra (Acts 14:19–20). For Paul, the fact he has physically suffered connects him to the crucifixion in a very real way. Paul therefore considers the scars on his body to be great honors because they prove he is suffering in the same way Jesus did (2 Cor 4:10). Douglas Moo draws a parallel to the mark of circumcision on which the opponents are insisting. They have their marks; Paul has been "branded for Jesus" by suffering for the gospel.[3]

---

3. Moo, *Galatians*, 404.

CONCLUSION

Paul's motivation for being a good ambassador for Christ is the love of God as demonstrated on the cross. Why do we participate in missions, either by helping to send people to a new location to preach the gospel or by going ourselves? What motivates us to be a part of the great adventure of missions?

QUESTIONS FOR FURTHER DISCUSSION

1. Paul's opponents were motivated to adopt some practices in order to avoid persecution. Is this a problem for contemporary Christians? What do we do in order to avoid shame and persecution today?
2. Paul is proud of the fact he has suffered for the sake of the gospel. What are some ways in which modern Christians have suffered?

Bibliography

Barrett, C. K. *Freedom and Obligation*. London: SPCK, 1985.
Bauckham, Richard. "Barnabas in Galatians." *JSNT* 2 (1979) 61–70.
Bauer, Walter, F. W. Danker, W. F. Arndt, and F. W. Gingrich. *A Greek-English Lexicon of the New Testament and Other Early Christian Literature*. 3rd ed. Chicago: University of Chicago Press, 2000.
Betz, Hans Dieter. *Galatians: A Commentary on Paul's Letter to the Churches in Galatia*. Hermeneia. Philadelphia: Fortress, 1979.
Bruce, F. F. *The Epistle to the Galatians*. NIGTC. Grand Rapids: Eerdmans, 1982.
Bundrick, David R. "Ta Stoicheia Tou Kosmou (Gal 4:3)." *JETS* 34 (1991) 353–64.
deSilva, David A. *The Letter to the Galatians*. NICNT. Grand Rapids: Eerdmans, 2018.
Dunn, James D. G. *Beginning from Jerusalem*. Grand Rapids: Eerdmans, 2009.
———. *The Epistle to the Galatians*. BNTC. Grand Rapids: Baker, 1993.
———. "The Incident at Antioch (Gal 2:11–18)." *Journal for the Study of the New Testament* 5 (1983) 3–57.
Fung, Ronald Y. K. *The Epistle to the Galatians*. NICNT. Grand Rapids: Eerdmans, 1988.
Jervis, L. Ann. *Galatians*. NIBC. Peabody, MA: Hendrickson, 1999.
Long, Phillip J. "A Brief Introduction to the New Perspective on Paul." *Journal of Grace Theology* 2.1 (2015) 3–18.
Martyn, J. Louis. *Galatians*. AB 33A. New York: Doubleday, 1997.
McKnight, Scot. *Galatians*. NIVAC. Grand Rapids: Zondervan, 1995.
Moo, Douglas J. *Galatians*. BECNT. Grand Rapids: Baker, 2012.
Nanos, Mark D. *The Galatians Debate: Contemporary Issues in Rhetorical and Historical Interpretation*. Peabody, MA: Hendrickson, 2002.
———. *The Irony of Galatians: Paul's Letter in First-Century Context*. Minneapolis: Fortress, 2002.
Oakes, Peter. *Galatians*. Paideia. Grands Rapids: Baker, 2015.
Schreiner, Thomas R. *Galatians*. ZECNT. Grand Rapids: Zondervan, 2010.
Silva, Moisés. *Interpreting Galatians: Explorations in Exegetical Method*. 2nd ed. Grand Rapids: Baker, 2001.
Winter, Bruce. *After Paul Left Corinth*. Grand Rapids: Eerdmans, 2001.

BIBLIOGRAPHY

Witherington, Ben. *The Acts of the Apostles: A Socio-Rhetorical Commentary.* Grand Rapids: Eerdmans, 2009.

———. *Grace in Galatia: A Commentary on St. Paul's Letter to the Galatians.* Grand Rapids: Eerdmans, 1998.

Wright, N. T. *The Climax of the Covenant: Christ and the Law in Pauline Theology.* London: T. & T. Clark, 1993.

———. *What Saint Paul Really Said: Was Paul of Tarsus the Real Founder of Christianity?* Grand Rapids: Eerdmans, 1997.

Young, Norman H. "PAIDAGOGOS: The Social Setting of a Pauline Metaphor." *Novum Testamentum* 29 (1987) 150–76.

www.ingramcontent.com/pod-product-compliance
Lightning Source LLC
Chambersburg PA
CBHW051937160426
43198CB00013B/2183